ACCLAIM FOR *CULTURE CODE CHAMPIONS*

"I've had the privilege to work with the millennial and Gen X generations for my entire career, and building a strong culture has been paramount in my success. Higgs' leadership formula for building dynamic teams will help you attract and keep all generations including the Gen Z folks who are just entering the workforce. By implementing the habits he provides, you will sell and perform better than your competition. Higgs' energy is infectious ... tap into it. Make this the business book your team reads together and implements!"

—Ken Hicks

CEO, Academy Sports
Former CEO, Foot Locker

"This is one of the most important books you will read on developing leadership skills through a focus on culture. I've studied the best coaches and teams in college sports and the winners have a tight-knit, branded culture they can rally around. The culture of continuous improvement and taking care of each other allows the team to perform in an extraordinary manner under intense pressure. We have many serious challenges in today's world. This book provides a plan and path to achievement by being inclusive and making heroes of others."

—Paul Finebaum

Television and Radio Personality, ESPN
New York Times *Best-Selling Author*

"When you think about making heroes as described in Culture Code Champions, *it might seem corny in the moment, but this is a very real human desire. Who doesn't want to be an Olympic gold medalist, a world-famous artist, or a revered business leader? These are meaningful accomplishments individually, but the real power is realized when a team of people collectively achieve a common goal. As people we want to not only be successful individually, but also to be part of something bigger than ourselves, part of a successful team so that those feelings of success and exhilaration that you get with achievement can be shared and appreciated with other people. That's where the culture of making heroes comes in. It's about getting every person on the broadest team you can imagine to be focused on doing everything they can do to make those around them a hero every day. When you create this culture, the power of positive momentum is unstoppable!*

"I had the good fortune to feel what it was like to work in this type of culture as a Mustanger for over seventeen years. I was part of a work family that believed in the talents of the people and created a culture that truly believed that, together, we could do anything. The real differentiator was the making heroes culture. Now, as the founder and CEO of a new business, my team is working to create that same culture and build the next $1 billion company filled with heroes using Bill's blueprint."

—Michele McNichol

Founder and CEO, Arion
Former CEO, Wood Group Mustang
Women Who Mean Business Award Recipient, 2018

"*I love reading books about people that actually make things happen ... especially around culture and values. Everyone has a culture ... it is how you get things done.* Culture Code Champions *is about creating a culture that positively changes people's lives. I have found that business success is all about people and creating an environment of trust and respect where folks want to do their very best every day. As we grew from a local to a national brand, our culture was twice as important as our strategy in maintaining our teams and delivering quality. This book is written by a man that makes it happen ... be it in the military, leading in the Boy Scouts, or in the field of business. In our world today, the truths in this book are needed now more than ever.*"

—David Weekley

Chairman, David Weekley Homes
National Builder of the Year Award, 1990 and 2013

"*Creating a great working environment invigorates people because they are working together as a team. In* Culture Code Champions, *Higgs correctly notes that people will have more energy, engage with their family, and help in the community because they enjoy their job. He was exposed to a strong culture as a young person in scouting and expanded that knowledge through experiences at West Point and in the US Army. I've watched Higgs continuously work to connect people and help them become overachievers. This book will help you do the same.*"

—Mark Turner

Scout Executive, Boy Scouts of America—Charlotte, North Carolina

"Culture Code Champions *provides a clear and concise formula to create a culture that delivers world-class team dynamics in any organization. We used these techniques to break down silos at NASA after the Columbia disaster as we undertook better communication, cross-training, and pushed the idea that we needed to make each other successful. Problem solving is always more about people than technology and Higgs shows how to win the hearts and minds of the team members to get better performance. I was confident in our team three years later when I gave the 'go for launch' command at the Kennedy Space Center. I highly recommend this book for anyone who wants to lead teams.*"

—Sandra C. Coleman

Space Shuttle External Tank Manager, NASA
Lifetime Achievement Award for Women in Aerospace, 2016

"Culture Code Champions *outlines exceptional tactics to build a world-class culture that is scalable and nimble enough to fit any size organization. I have used these leadership principles in both the US Air Force and multiple* Fortune *100 companies ... your people will be happy, more productive and drive success. Hiring right, putting your people first and building a rock-solid culture seems basic. However, when leading large teams of people, it can become complex very quickly. Take notes in the margins and put this knowledge to work!*"

—Jason Mock

United States Air Force Academy, 1996
Senior Vice President, Consumer Bank at Bank of America

"I am not a Mustanger. Or maybe I am. I was Bill's 'client,' before Mustang started. As a young project supervisor for ARCO, we connected on several key ideas—all of which have made my success—and all of which you will get from this book. Here are a few examples and questions Bill answers:

- **Be ruthlessly selfish about attracting the best talent:** *The best teams are made up of the best people—how do you attract them? How do you retain them in both up and down markets?*

- **The best player plays:** *The best projects and company formations occur right at the intersection of clients, contractors, and supplier/vendors. How best to integrate them and break down the silos?*

- **The upside down organizational chart:** *When Bill's Mustang team was doing the topsides engineering for Atlantis in an overheated market (2002–2006), it was easy to see that we needed the very best from my BP team, Mustang, and all of our critical suppliers. The best are always hard to recruit and retain—they are all essentially 'volunteers'— they can work anywhere they want. How do you make your business or project the one that everyone wants to join?*

"Whether you are building a company or a project team, you will find something you can put to immediate use on every page in Culture Code Champions."

—Gregory Sills

President, Leading Projects LLC
Formerly EVP and Chief Development Officer, Cobalt
VP Major Projects, BP and Marathon

CULTURE CODE

CODE

CHAMPIONS

BILL HIGGS

CULTURE CODE CHAMPIONS

7 Steps To Scale & Succeed In Your Business

ForbesBooks

Published by ForbesBooks, Charleston, South Carolina.
Member of Advantage Media Group.

ForbesBooks is a registered trademark, and the ForbesBooks colophon is a trademark of Forbes Media, LLC.

Printed in the United States of America.

10 9 8 7 6 5 4 3 2 1

ISBN: 978-1-946633-69-9

Book design by Wendy Stevens

This publication is designed to provide accurate and authoritative information in regard to the subject matter covered. It is sold with the understanding that the publisher is not engaged in rendering legal, accounting, or other professional services. If legal advice or other expert assistance is required, the services of a competent professional person should be sought.

Advantage Media Group is proud to be a part of the Tree Neutral® program. Tree Neutral offsets the number of trees consumed in the production and printing of this book by taking proactive steps such as planting trees in direct proportion to the number of trees used to print books. To learn more about Tree Neutral, please visit **www.treeneutral.com**.

Since 1917, the Forbes mission has remained constant. Global Champions of Entrepreneurial Capitalism. ForbesBooks exists to further that aim by bringing the Stories, Passion, and Knowledge of top thought leaders to the forefront. ForbesBooks brings you The Best in Business. To be considered for publication, please visit **www.forbesbooks.com**.

This book is dedicated to those who want to improve their ability to help other people enjoy their work environment more—to people who want to spiral up attitudes in an organization so that it prospers and everyone can take that positive attitude and energy home and into the community.

Culture Code Champions grew out of all the amazing people
that I have had the privilege to serve at the company
I cofounded called Mustang.

Mustang Vision Statement

*Our quest is to embody a culture that inspires super motivated people to
make Heroes of clients, partners, vendors, and Mustangers!*

PREFACE ON CULTURE

The army culture is built around the warrior ethos of mission first, never accepting defeat, never quitting and never leaving a fallen comrade behind. *Culture Code Champions* grew out of this team-first mentality. The Ranger Creed takes this cultural foundation a step further and is summarized in the motto "Rangers lead the way!" In the following story and testimonial you will see how the Task Force Ranger culture trumps the strategy and plan to win the day in the heat of battle.

Lee A. Van Arsdale is one of my West Point classmates and one of my personal heroes. This is his experience from The Battle of Mogadishu—the events of which were the basis for the book and movie *Black Hawk Down*. Moving the combat units from the crash site to the rally point and then out of Mogadishu famously constitutes the "Mogadishu Mile" (although it was more like three miles).

—Bill Higgs

Lee:

In the late summer and fall of 1993 I was a member of Task Force (TF) Ranger in Mogadishu, Somalia. TF Ranger was comprised of elements of the 75th Ranger Regiment, the 160th Special Operations Aviation Regiment, an Army Special Mission Unit, and a headquarters element. Our mission was straightforward: capture or kill General Mohammed Farah Aidid, a warlord in command of the Habr Gedr clan militia. They were responsible for the deaths of over 20 Pakistani peacekeepers sent to Somalia as part of a United Nations effort to cease the starvation caused by the Somali civil war. The Pakistanis were ambushed in June, and TF Ranger trained and rehearsed for two months until deploying in August.

General Aidid had not been seen since June, and in order to carry out our mission the one piece of critical intelligence was the target's location. Knowing this, we planned to systematically roll up Aidid's infrastructure, thereby depriving him of the people and things he needed, eventually driving him to the surface. From August to October we did just that, successfully executing six missions, such as capturing his chief financier, and taking out the radio station he was using to direct his militia.

Then, on October 3rd, we received actionable intelligence that two of Aidid's lieutenants would be conducting a personal meeting. This was precisely the type of target that fit with our strategy. Complicating things was the fact that the meet would take place in a walled compound with multistoried buildings. We had no way of knowing where in the compound the meet would take place, and each lieutenant traveled with about a dozen well-armed bodyguards.

TF Ranger's culture was built around reacting quickly in all phases of a mission. Our process used a number of templates that were available for every mission set. When a mission came down it was a simple matter of selecting the proper template, making any last minute adjustments, and then executing.

The planning had been ongoing since the June massacre, and included not just the basic plan but contingencies for logical occurrences. While we were constrained in our manpower and number of helicopters and vehicles, for us those constraints were planning factors. When a plan was formulated, a brief back was conducted so the commander could approve, amend, or send it back to the drawing board, and ensure everyone was on the same page.

Prior to deployment every rehearsal was followed by what we called a hotwash, or after action review. This forum allowed every participant to give their perspective on how the plan could be improved, and further served as a way to keep everyone on the same page. In Somalia, every mission was likewise followed up with a hotwash.

Our plan on October 3rd was for the Special Mission Unit (SMU) assault force to take down the compound and arrest the lieutenants, while the Rangers provided security around the target. Both elements would be transported by 160th helicopters, conduct the mission, and then exfiltrate the area via a vehicular convoy on standby in an adjacent neighborhood.

The operation went according to plan, and was absolutely textbook in execution. The lieutenants were captured and the bodyguards were all flex cuffed so they were no longer a threat. While waiting for the four Ranger elements to collapse onto the compound so the entire element could exfiltrate together, one of the circling Blackhawk helicopters, piloted by my friend Cliff Wolcott, was shot down. In the words of Major General Bill Garrison, the TF Ranger commander, "We just lost the initiative."

With a clan militia estimated at 3,000 fighters, and an on-ground TF Ranger element of less than 100, maintaining the initiative was crucial to our success. We immediately implemented our contingency plans when the helicopter, call sign Super 61, went down. One of the contingencies was to dispatch the Search and Rescue (SAR) helicopter to the crash site, while General Garrison simultaneously called for our Quick Reaction Force (QRF), the US Army 10th Mountain Division, in Somalia as part of the United Nations mission.

This is where our culture took over. We executed a contingency that wasn't planned for: the nearest Ranger element to the crash site saw the bird go down, and immediately ran there. Super 61 went down in a bad neighborhood, and we all knew that the militia would be eager to get there first, and we were determined that we would win that race!

The SAR bird and Rangers got to Super 61 at about the same time, just ahead of the militia, thanks to the heroic efforts of Dan Busch. Dan was a SMU sniper on Super 61, and single-handedly held off the first militia members to arrive at the scene. Dan was mortally wounded, but held the militia at bay just long enough.

Meanwhile, the QRF arrived at the TF Ranger Joint Operations Center (JOC) from their location and got a quick update on the situation. At this time I was in the JOC, and as the QRF was departing for the crash site, General Garrison turned to me and said simply "Go with them." Such was the nature of our relationship and the culture we came from, built on integrity and trust, that nothing else was necessary. I knew that my charter was to develop the situation as necessary to get our troops at the crash site—by now the assault force and entire Ranger security element, encircled by the militia—safely back to our base.

The QRF was ambushed shortly after leaving the base, and we were in totally unarmored vehicles. Circumstances precluded us from driving through the ambush, and our lack of armor left us completely vulnerable. The QRF commander, or someone higher in his chain of command, I'm not sure which, decided to return to base and regroup. We did just that, and later in the evening we were ready for take two, this time with Pakistani tanks and Malaysian Armored Personnel Carriers (APCs).

By now we had two downed helicopters, and our plan was to move to a rally point roughly equidistant between the crash sites. From there one 10th Mountain Division Company (about 100 soldiers) would go to each crash site, and one company would remain at the rally point as a reserve. I decided to accompany the unit going to the Super 61 crash site, as that's where all of the TF Ranger elements were located, still holding off the militia. Given the situation—nighttime, blinding dust, continuous noise, automatic weapons fire, explosions, and a group of soldiers moving through the streets to where another group of soldiers was holding ground—I figured my top priority was avoiding accidental fratricide.

I rode to the rally point in a Malaysian APC with a couple of SMU colleagues, where we dismounted in order to dismantle a flaming roadblock. I'd have been perfectly happy to remain in the APC all the way to the crash site, but the roadblocks and militia presence precluded that. As it was, the dismounted element and APCs provided each other mutual support, and in that manner we moved out. I positioned myself in the middle of the company with the SMU men, thinking that if we were needed somewhere that was the best place from which to react.

About halfway there we took significant fire from a multi-story building and got held up. We quickly rectified the situation, but lost our momentum. The company commander, Captain Drew Meyerowich, told me that the APCs refused to go any further, and he couldn't proceed without them. I told one of the SMU soldiers, Matt Rierson, to get in the lead APC and make it move forward. I then moved to the front of the line of soldiers and told them to follow me. Even though I wasn't in their chain of command and they didn't know who I was, I knew without a doubt that these American soldiers would respond to positive leadership. Without delay the APCs and dismounted soldiers both began moving.

When we neared the crash site, I halted the element and moved forward with my Radio-Telephone Operator (RTO) Bob Kingman. I was in radio contact with the assault force commander, Captain Scott Miller, and met with him face to face prior to bringing up the entire QRF. Scott gave me a run down on where the TF Ranger elements were located, which allowed us to fold the QRF into the perimeter without any drama.

At this time I turned my attention to the matter of extricating the pilot's and copilot's bodies from the wreckage. When their aircraft was hit they did everything exactly right in order to save the four snipers and two crew chiefs in back, but did so at the sacrifice of their own lives. They were now trapped in the wreckage, and it was our intent that we not leave without them. Fortunately we weren't taking any casualties at the time, so we were able to spend the time it took to finally get them out.

By now it was daylight, and we needed to get back to the rally point. The APCs that accompanied us to the crash site were now full with our wounded comrades, so once again it wasn't a simple matter of riding to the destination in an APC. I put the 10th Mountain Division in the lead, as they were the freshest and knew the way. I put the SMU element in the middle again, as they were the most experienced and could react to wherever they may be needed. The Rangers brought up the rear, and though many of them were exhausted and dehydrated, they were still Rangers and I felt good with them protecting the rear.

We returned to the rally point without incident, and I received a report from every subordinate leader that all their men were accounted for. Only then did I give the order to load up the vehicles.

Scott Miller and I were the last to load up, along with our RTOs, and we proceeded back without further incident.

Seventeen brave Americans lost their lives during that fight, and two days later Matt Rierson was killed in a mortar attack on our base. Even though there was a tragic loss of life—18 Americans and an estimated 1,000 militia, *we accomplished the mission we were tasked with that day*, and completely eviscerated the Habr Gedr militia.

Not every day in my Army life was quite as action-packed as this, but I did apply leadership and culture building principles every day, all of which are reinforced in *Culture Code Champions*.

From a cultural aspect, the right team will always find a way to succeed, no matter what happens. The wrong team, even if it is properly resourced and has everything it needs to succeed, will seldom achieve complete success.

Twice now I've had the opportunity to lead companies as the chief executive officer. In both instances we were able to achieve good success, and I attribute that in no small part to the leadership and culture building lessons I learned in the army. In my experience, army leadership is the same as business leadership—in both cases you're leading people. Higgs' book *Culture Code Champions* is a terrific blend of military leadership, culture and ethos applied to very effective business practices.

—Lee A. Van Arsdale

LTC, Task Force Ranger
Black Hawk Down Mission/Rescue
Former CEO, Triple Canopy

FOREWORD

The West Point Class of 1974 produced more senior military officers than almost any class in its 216-year history. Less well known, but equally important in its contribution to our society, is the fact that it produced as many or more senior business executives, innovators, and entrepreneurs. Among all of these leaders, Bill Higgs stands out.

At West Point, Bill was a leader among our group of leaders-in-waiting. We spent four years together learning to understand and appreciate the values we each applied later to our chosen professions. Even then, Bill's character, integrity, work ethic, and genuine concern for the people around him was evident. In the forty-five years from the time I entered West Point in 1970 to when I retired from the military in 2015 as our nation's highest-ranking military officer, I got to know and evaluate many leaders. I don't throw the word "charismatic" around loosely in describing them. Bill Higgs was charismatic.

We've stayed in touch over those forty-five years and especially during the last twenty as we committed to continuing to learn even as we continued to lead. That's why Bill's book is so important and timely. It's not just a personal success story; it's a template for successful leaders who want to remain successful.

In his new book *Culture Code Champions*, Bill describes his leadership journey as co-founder of Mustang Engineering, a company that grew from three people and a $15,000 investment to 6,500 people and $1 billion in annual revenues in only twenty years. He deftly and interestingly weaves a story about the intersection of people and projects, that point where leaders work to balance time schedules, the bottom line, and the human dimension of business to create a successful and enduring culture.

Bill argues with conviction that the key to becoming successful and staying successful is in expanding the idea of "team" to include employees, leaders, suppliers, and customers. Other books have made the point that teamwork and reputation matter; Bill Higgs' anecdotes and vignettes bring it to life persuasively.

Among many valuable contributions to leadership theory, Bill's assertion in *Culture Code Champions* that the better we do, the more we should give back to the community may be the most valuable. Our most basic instinct—on the job and off—is to feel a sense of belonging and to believe our contributions matter. In his chapter on giving back, Bill makes a pragmatic case that giving back is both important for the community but also an important part of building a company's culture.

Bill Higgs has something to say, the experience to back it up, and stories to bring it to life. If you're serious about learning to lead, this is a book you won't want to end.

—Martin Dempsey
Retired US General
18th Chairman, Joint Chiefs of Staff
Chairman, USA Basketball

CONTENTS

MAKING HEROES IS VITAL TO CULTURE CODE CHAMPIONS

Y ou can change lives by creating an energetic, positive work environment that spirals people's attitudes up, and this book will show you how. You have never heard of Mustang Engineering, Inc., but that doesn't matter; the company and industry are immaterial. The culture it built stands the test of time.

It was started during a severe industry downturn in a mundane, highly competitive services industry where people go home every night and can leave for another job the next day. By the time Mustang was started, hundreds of other companies in the industry had come and gone with the industry cycles, never getting larger than eighty people. The severe cycles eliminated any loyalty between companies and people.

This is a different type of business book in that it focuses on how one company created a high-performance team culture that worked across all aspects of the company, from HR to sales to operations to strategic planning to legal and financial reporting. Basic building blocks of this culture were adapted from my experiences at West Point, in Army Ranger School, and as a combat engineer company commander. My partners brought their experiences from the tight-knit cultures of Texas A&M and Texas A&I along with their natural collaborative nature. Our inclusive team culture was strong enough and dynamic enough that it changed a large portion of our industry from win-lose contracting to win-win cooperation.

This book will show you how to build or change a culture. In 1987, we founded our firm with the idea of creating a better kind of company. I was thirty-five years old; one of my co-founders, Paul Redmon, was a few years younger than I; the other, Felix Covington, was a few years older. None of us made the decision lightly: we planned and mulled for two years before pulling the trigger, but once we did, we never looked back.

In the early days, we hoped our $15,000 investment would grow to a thirty-five-person company. Twenty years later, when we retired, Mustang was a billion-dollar company with more than 6,500 people in offices around the world. Four years later the 2nd and 3rd generation leadership grew it to $2 billion in annual revenues and 12,000 people. *Inc. Magazine* cited us as one of the "Inc. 500 fastest-growing companies in America"—for two straight years—and we were the top-ranked technical firm in North America. We achieved this by putting simple, common-sense principles to work.

That kind of success is very rare: *only six out of one million start-ups grow to become billion-dollar businesses.* We believe we achieved this level of success because of the *culture* of the organization we created.

You read that right: because of the *culture*—that touchy-feely intangible quality that so many companies don't put energy into. We did—and the habits that created the culture live on, long after the founders left the company, because our people embraced those habits for creating an environment they did not want to lose.

Mustang's culture grew even stronger, from bottom to top in the organization, after we left in 2008. In 2016, the team put out a video of people in eight offices around the world saying in their own language what it meant to be a Mustanger (our moniker). Our vision was to "Make Heroes" of our suppliers, clients, and other Mustangers (i.e., to make them successful)—and that came through. The English subtitles in the video matched the words and phrases we had used in our fourth year. It was hard to imagine this would ever happen in an industry that did not treat service organizations well. Culture is how you get things done; we wanted to get things done through great team dynamics in all actions.

I believe the basic building blocks of our culture can help other organizations, too, no matter what business you're in, or what the purpose of your organization is, even if it's not a business. My first book, *Mustang, the Story—from Zero to $1 Billion*, told the history of how Paul, Felix, and I started and grew our business, but I wrote that book chronologically, and its focus is very much on the oil industry. In it, I discussed hiring, firing, contracting, organization structure, and culture. However, people who don't work in the oil industry may have to dig in to find *general* business ideas that can help them. This book pulls out the gold-nugget business ideas and organizes them around building a team culture. We were recognized as the "Kings of Culture" in our industry for building a company where loyalty and taking care of people reigns supreme and I want to pass that on, in *Culture Code Champions*.

The company changed the lives of its people (Mustangers), their families, the vendors and clients they served, and the communities where they lived. This resulted from creating an energetic, positive work environment that spirals people's attitudes up. All the people who felt they were blessed to be touched by Mustang want the story told in a manner that will allow other companies and organizations to copy the habits that created an unbelievable destiny.

The seven simple steps and habits we created are now being used by groups of Mustangers that have moved to other companies and are effectively changing those companies in an impactful way. There are many Mustang-type cultures out there now!

As you read this book, think about how you could tweak what we did to match your organization. It has to be authentic and needs to come from the heart, or it will not become a habit and your people will not perpetuate it for your sake or theirs.

Culture will help you create a "cycle-proof" company like ours:

GROWTH THROUGH 4 BUST CYCLES TAKES LEADERSHIP AT ALL LEVELS

If you're the CEO of a global *Fortune* 500 organization or the owner of a company, this book is for you.

If you are in HR and tasked with building a culture or in sales and tasked with building a brand, this book is for you.

If you're a senior manager or someone who manages or supervises others—even if it's only one person—this book is for you.

If you aspire to lead a *Fortune* 500 company, or a division or department within a large organization, or if you're a would-be entrepreneur and you want to start your own business, this book is for you.

And if you're the leader of a scout troop; a church group; or, in fact, any other organization or community group, this book is for you.

Why? Because the fundamental principle explained in the following pages is that *people* are the crux of any organization's success.

This book devotes a chapter to each of the main building blocks of Mustang's team-building success—which can be *your* success, too.

- Chapter 1 describes how to **hire the right people**: how to find people that will fit your culture and how to retain and motivate them, so they'll stay for the long term. Good people are *not* a dime a dozen; they're the key to your organization's success.

- Chapter 2 describes how to **create a culture that establishes your organization's unique identity.** Creating a spirit of belonging is the key to your brand, that your people will rally around, and which will differentiate you from anyone else.

- Chapter 3 discusses how to ***sell your products or services,*** because the first priority of every business is sales. You need to be able to sell what you do or make to provide job security and allow your culture to blossom.

- Chapter 4 focuses on how to ***bust the silos*** that plague all organizations, so you can get your people to work together as a high-functioning team.

- Chapter 5 picks up on the theme of teamwork and describes how to ***improve communication*** inside your organization as well as with clients and vendors—because *all* problems are communication problems.

- Chapter 6 covers how to ***execute efficiently and productively*** by streamlining the way you manage tasks and by creating repeatable processes.

- Finally, Chapter 7 encourages you to ***give back to your community,*** because life isn't all about work, and once you've achieved the level of success I describe in the first six chapters, you'll want to do whatever you can to help others.

• • •

The army taught me how much fun it is to work with high-performing, hand-picked teams, and I wanted to continue to have those experiences in my civilian working life. Although I learned an enormous amount from my early bosses and mentors, that "team spirit" was missing. I felt then—and still feel now—that great teamwork is the key to organizational success and contributes greatly to personal happiness. That's why I've written this book: to help *you* make heroes of everyone you work with. Let's go make heroes and make your culture count!

WORKSHEETS

SWOT analysis worksheets are provided after each chapter to help you evaluate your company, organization or team. SWOT is shorthand for strengths, weaknesses, opportunities and threats.

The quick SWOT analysis helps you and others understand how something is performing and what challenges could stand in the way of success. The strengths and weaknesses sections focus on internal influences, while the opportunities and threats look at external factors.

Remember to be very objective and ruthlessly honest when inputting to the worksheet. You will also find it beneficial to get other people's input through discussion.

Refer to the topic at the top of the worksheet and fill in the spaces based on that topic. Here are the questions you are working to answer for each section:

Strengths: Where do you excel compared to competitors?

Weaknesses: Where are you behind competitors, or where you want to be?

Opportunities: What external factor could help you get a competitive advantage?

Threats: What external factor could jeopardize your success?

OBJECTIVE:

Join me in learning how to create Culture Code Champions and build the organization that top people want to join. You will improve your bottom line by reducing turnover and increasing efficiency.

CULTURE CODE CHAMPIONS WORKSHEET:
CURRENT CULTURE SWOT

STRENGTH:
Internal:_____

_____

_____

_____

WEAKNESS:
Internal:_____

_____

_____

_____

OPPORTUNITY:
External:_____

_____

_____

_____

THREAT:
External:_____

_____

_____

_____

SWOT Your Culture Killers!

CHAPTER 1

HIRE RIGHT: CONTINUOUSLY RECRUIT TOP TALENT

Hiring the right people to fit your organization's culture and treating them right is *the most important key to your organization's success*. Unfortunately, many companies and organizations give lip service to that idea, but they don't practice what they preach—which, naturally, results in good people leaving for better opportunities where they will be valued and respected. Many other companies don't even bother to pretend that they value their people: they believe that people are expendable, that they're replaceable, that if someone doesn't work out in a particular job or capacity—or if that person leaves to go elsewhere—that it will be easy to find someone else just as good, if not better.

I disagree; Mustang proved that's not true at all.

Mustang has had people stay for twenty-plus years—which was previously unheard of on the contractor side of the oil industry (and may also be unheard of in *your* industry or operation). That's an impressive number when you keep in mind that Mustang was founded only thirty-three years ago (at the time of this writing in 2020)—which means that many of our people have been with us almost from the beginning.

Moreover, our turnover rate of employees was amazingly low. The typical turnover rate in our industry was 35 percent—which means that one out of three people leave a company *every year,* whereas Mustang's turnover rate was less than 5 percent. That's almost unbelievable—except that it's true. That low level of turnover makes work much easier, because the longer people work together, the more comfortable they are with each other, the more shared knowledge and experience they bring to each new project, and then projects can get done faster and more efficiently.

> *Note: I use the term "project," but it could be an initiative or a task or any other kind of job. Everything being done in business and in organizations is one of these. They consist of a plan with a concept, execution, end, and evaluation.*

The most quantifiable costs result from turnover, training new people, poor handoffs between people due to communication, rework and losing clients either in the bid process or after working with them. The cost is easily 2–3 percent off of your bottom line profit or your other key performance indicators (KPIs). For example, if your bottom line is 6 percent net profit, it could be 8–9 percent after implementing the *Culture Code Champions 7: Steps to Scale and Succeed in Your Business.*

What is your <u>current</u> culture costing you? Go to culturecode-champions.com to fill out the CCC Assessment and the Culture Cost Calculator for your organization. With these results in hand, the thoughts and actions supplied in this book will ring true to you and spur you to implement a variation that matches your team. As you read, take notes on your printout of the CCC Culture Assessment in the areas where you were weak or a strength that you want to make stronger. The goal is to deliver the additional bottom line you arrived at with the Culture Cost Calculator.

The 7 steps actually added 15 percent to our bottom line compared to our competitors, while significantly improving the quality of life for our people and their families.

From our earliest days in business, we saw the rewards of low turnover. At the end of our second year in business, we were already working with some of the "majors" in the oil industry—Amoco, Conoco, ARCO, Shell, Marathon, and BP—because they saw that our turnover was low. They could feel the camaraderie and team spirit in our people, and they were impressed that although we were small, we had worked on some large oil platforms in the Gulf of Mexico. The confidence from those companies—and the projects they hired us to work on—helped our fledgling company enormously.

So how do you find the "absolute best people" to work with? If you're good enough, they'll find you! Of course, to make that happen, you have to establish that your organization is one that people will want to work for. I'll discuss that in detail in the next chapter, which covers how to create—and maintain—a team culture where people will be happy (yes, *happy*) to work. Now, let me give you some suggestions on how to find and keep people you'll want to work with.

REFERRAL HIRING: "OPERATION HORSETHIEF"

Every industry is tight-knit. In any city or region, all the companies or organizations that are in the same business or industry (and are competing with each other) know who the good people are—and where they are.

From the beginning, we decided not to strip our previous employer of good people, which is what a lot of companies do, especially if the founders of the new company have all come from the same former company (as we had). We held no grudge against our previous company; we simply wanted to create our own job security during a severe industry downturn (1982–1992). Poaching talent from our former employer just seemed wrong to us.

Keeping our eyes and ears open, we found good people who *needed* jobs due to layoffs or company closures. For example, during our first few weeks, we bought most of our furniture from other engineering firms that were closing due to the low oil prices. (Frugality was critical, as our nest egg was only $15,000.) We talked to the companies that were going out of business to find out who were their best people, and where did they go? This was a very effective way to get a jump start on hiring, because it's very difficult, almost impossible, to just read a resume and interview a candidate and know you're hiring someone who can perform at a high level every day. The honest referrals helped us find great talent.

Then, once you have a few outstanding people working for you, all you need to do is tap into *their* networks. This is a good way to find the best people: simply ask the valued people who already work with you, *who else they know* who might want to work for your organization.

This was the start of what we affectionately called "Operation Horsethief" (tying in, of course, to our Mustang horse theme). Identify the horses wherever they are and go get them. The fun name kept recruiting in the front of our people's minds. Continuous recruiting in good times and bad is critical to a strong culture.

For years, this type of recruiting worked well. Although it might seem obvious to anyone reading this book, I continue to be surprised at how many companies and organizations *don't* do this. Why look *outside* your organization when your *insiders* already have a network of talented contacts you can draw on?

So, we encouraged all our people to recommend friends and former colleagues to us. And, of course they did, because they

TO FIND THE BEST PEOPLE: ASK THE VALUED PEOPLE WHO ALREADY WORK WITH YOU, *WHO ELSE THEY KNOW* WHO MIGHT WANT TO WORK FOR YOUR ORGANIZATION.

wanted to help others find jobs at the company *they* enjoyed working for. We didn't even offer incentives to do this. In fact, for the first seven years we were in business, we did *all* our hiring this way. We never advertised anywhere, and only did some referral hiring with a finder's fee in year 8, due to an influx of work. Here's how quickly we grew:

- Day 1: The 3 cofounders

- End of Year 1: 48 people

- Year 4: 200 people

- Year 5: 280 people

- Year 8: 450 people

- Year 13: 1,000 people

That's a lot of growth, and very fast! Yet, as mentioned, it wasn't until our eighth year when our workload increased substantially and suddenly that we offered a finder's fee. At that point, we had about 450 people, but in the next year, we added 150 more. To meet that staffing need, we offered a $500 finder's fee to our people, if they brought in good talent that stayed a minimum of six months. Our hope was that if the new hires could survive our company's trial-by-fire breakneck pace during the first six months, they would likely stay with us for the long haul. Fortunately, we only had to use a finder's fee for a short time.

When we went back to referral hiring (Operation Horsethief) without a finder's fee, our people understood. They appreciated the perk while it lasted, and they trusted that the owners would take care of them in other ways—and they were right!

"HORSETHIEF" HIRING PROVIDED LASTING RESULTS

For those of you who think it's unfair to your competitors to pull their best people away from them, keep in mind that those people wouldn't be leaving those organizations—or considering leaving—if they were completely content where they were. You're not *kidnapping* people or forcing them to work for you: you're simply *inviting* them. When they know that your organization is successful, and that you treat your people well, they'll want to come join you.

There were a few times that we got a call from another company after Mustang had hired one of its top performers. Whenever I got one of those calls, I gently told the unhappy manager on the other end of the line, "You know, your job was to make sure that person was happy and content and wanted to continue working for your company. Somehow, you failed in doing that. The person we hired *wanted* to move. Even if you give that person an increase in pay or better benefits or some other perk, you will still have somebody you're not connecting with for some reason."

That is how we hired our first structural engineering manager, John Ellis, who came from a competitor where he was the number two person in the structural department. John wanted to leave, because the manager was only two years older, and John realized he was never going to get that position. We brought him over to our company, and he flourished; in fact, (as of 2020) he's still at Mustang after twenty-nine years.

WHEN THEY KNOW THAT YOUR ORGANIZATION IS SUCCESSFUL, AND THAT YOU TREAT YOUR PEOPLE WELL, THEY'LL WANT TO COME JOIN YOU.

Later, Ken Comeaux was hired based on strong recommendations from our electrical designers. It was a bit of a challenge to persuade him to move his young family from Louisiana to Houston to manage a group of four electrical engineers and ten designers. But he came, and his responsibilities grew with us: eventually, his department was 350 people, and he stayed with the company for twenty-four years.

Another great example was picking up Randy Hewett, who had been laid off and was hired to do scheduling for us. After a few years, he realized that Mustang was getting into much bigger and more complex projects than he was comfortable doing. He knew that Randy Alton, whom he had worked with, had all the expertise and connections to take Mustang where it needed to go. He hired Alton, even though he knew that Alton would take his job as manager of the scheduling group. That's pretty cool. Alton gave us ten good years, and Hewett retired from Mustang after twenty years.

In 2000, Dena Lee came in to head up marketing from Kellogg Brown & Root (KBR, a world-class engineering and construction company) on the recommendation of Mike Farley, who had worked with her. Mike had come from KBR and totally loved the pace of Mustang. He was confident Dena would feel the same. After three months, I asked Dena how things were going. She said her first ninety days had been like stepping off of a super-tanker and onto a speedboat … and that she was totally immersed and loving it. Dena stayed for seventeen years and helped us expand worldwide.

These few examples show the strength of referral hiring through Operation Horsethief: top quality people who stayed, flourished, and grew with the company.

Our hiring method also created significant savings to our bottom line in two ways. First, most companies hire four to six people for every "keeper" (someone who stays two years) they find. This churning of people makes your existing team less efficient as they have to train and sort through them. Secondly, our people did not leave, because they knew and liked whomever recruited them, or because they had tried hard for quite a while to get in the door at Mustang. They knew we were selective!

It is important to point out that we hired people with long-term intent. We lost some people who were poached with the lure of a signing bonus and an unrealistically high hourly pay rate at one of the big firms. These people were happy at Mustang but could not turn down the cash for their family. They either did not realize or were misled, but it was not sustainable work, and they were laid off and looking for a job in a few months. We brought most of them back. They had learned that the hiring company was just in a short-term bind and took advantage of them. None of us liked seeing this happen to people in boom times.

Again, the concept of "thieving" was used in jest—another way of thinking about the common current concept of being a "talent magnet." In reality, we were creating an internal culture that had a far-reaching reputation. The best people in the industry were looking for a way in, even in the early days, and all that was needed was connecting the dots. Trust me: there are not enough employment incentives in the world to create a sustainable influx of talented people into a toxic and failing entity!

• • •

The oil industry is one of extreme booms and busts, and many of the companies working in that industry couldn't survive its wild swings. As a result, there were always companies going out of business— through no fault of the smart, talented people who worked there. Those people still needed jobs and a way to earn a living, so by picking them up and hiring them for Mustang, we created a win-win situation for a lot of terrific people.

Our first direct hire at Mustang, in 1987, was a piping designer named Divakar Pathak. He came to our attention as we were moving some office furniture from the engineering firm he had worked for, which was closing. Divakar had a family to support, so he had taken a job selling cars at a nearby dealership. He was excited to get our call asking him to come in for an interview. Four other people from Divakar's previous company also joined Mustang. But even more impressive is the fact that Divakar is still with the company as I write this.

In the category of "what goes around comes around," we found that it is good business to develop a reputation for helping people find jobs at other firms, even when you're not hiring. This was also something we did to help people, and it paid dividends for us many times due to the goodwill we created in the industry.

For example, Jim Linder from Transco Exploration (a division of Transco Energy, which was primarily a pipeline company) called to let us know he had just been laid off, and he was wondering if we might know anyone who was looking for someone with his experience and background. By this time, we were known in the industry to be solidly wired in to a wide variety of companies, so this call wasn't surprising. Jim came in for an interview, figuring he had nothing to lose since he wasn't working, and he had everything to gain, because maybe we'd know a company that would benefit from his background. As it happened, Jim was exactly what our company needed: a construction guy to head up our inspection group. He interviewed well, we could tell he would fit with our culture, and we hired him.

Don't be shy about looking at the companies *you've* worked for in the past, to see if anyone else wants to move on. If you've worked with them directly, you already know their work habits and personalities, so that removes some of the unknowns from the hiring process. This may sound like "Hiring 101," but again, I continue to be amazed when I talk to business leaders and department managers in a wide variety of industries who *don't* do this. They figure they have an entire Human Resources department to advertise for candidates, review the mountain of resumes that inevitably come in, conduct initial interviews to screen for the best possible matches for the job in question, and then recommend a select few to the hiring manager.

But what do you do if you don't have a huge HR department? Or *any* HR department? At Mustang, we were so busy growing our business, finding new clients, and working on projects, that no professional worked full time in HR for the first ten years we were in business! You read that right: in fact, I was still doing the payroll (in addition to my other engineering, sales, and management responsibilities) when the company had grown to 450 employees. In hindsight, someone should have been brought in much sooner than our tenth year to handle human resources. After we hired our first HR manager, we realized just how much we had needed them. My point, however, is that even if you *do* have someone who handles HR, you can still often find great people just by thinking about whom you've worked with in the past who might be a good fit for your organization.

That happened to us when we hired our first engineer, Don Leinweber, five months after starting the company. My partner, Paul, was doing an enormous amount of work: all the structural engineering, 70 percent of the mechanical engineering, 80 percent of the project management, 30 percent of the proposal writing, 20 percent of the sales calls, and 100 percent of the hiring—as well as developing all our technical standards, approving all our time sheets and expense reports, and leading the company as we were growing so quickly. As a result—and quite understandably—he was desperate to find someone who could handle some of the engineering work.

When Paul got a call from a former colleague, he was excited to hear that Don was interested in making a move. Because it was so critical to hire someone, my two cofounders and I agreed to forego taking a paycheck for another three months so that we could hire Don. That was a tough decision for all of us and our families, since we had already gone three months without pay. But we also knew we needed to grow the number of people working for us, or our company would go under just from the sheer weight of the workload. Six months without pay would be our "sweat equity" investment in the startup of Mustang. So, we tightened our belts some more and hired our first engineer.

Even if you're not running a small business or starting your own business, you should think like an entrepreneur. Don't offload responsibilities—like hiring—to someone else if you can spend a little bit of time thinking creatively about where you can find good people. Sometimes, just a few minutes of mining your memory bank and your personal network can pay off for everyone involved!

JOB-PLACEMENT AGENCIES CAN BE YOUR HR GROUP FOR SCREENING

Thinking like entrepreneurs led us to sign exclusive contracts with three job-placement agencies to help us screen for quality people. In return for this exclusivity, we asked them to finance our payroll until we were paid by our clients. They agreed, as long as they were able to approve the clients based on their experience. This solved our main cash-flow problem, because banks would not help a startup in the oil business. These agencies had complained that they could not get anyone to *leave* Mustang, so they were challenged to find Mustangers to join us in order to earn their money. They knew the quality and type of collaborative people our company wanted, because they were familiar with the people already working for us.

Even when we were not looking for people, sometimes these agencies would call saying, "We have found a Mustanger for you!" This quality of person does not come available all the time because they are strong team players and the agencies knew when they had one. Since we knew the screening was top rate, those people were always hired. The agencies performed a critical part of our HR function for us.

VARIETY OF OPPORTUNITY HELPS IN RECRUITING

The company was made up of many types of multidiscipline teams with various strengths. This allowed us to match the type of work to a person's interests. There were teams for small projects, large projects, onshore, offshore, pipeline, automation, etc. We kept these teams together long term and rotated people among them to cross-train. Eventually, we would launch a new team with some of the original team's strongest people. This history of growing people's skills helped us recruit, as we could tailor the job and team to match a new person's temperament and interests. The cross-training and potential to grow into new teams helped us retain people long term.

CREATING JOB SECURITY THROUGH THE "JOB ON THE CORNER OF THE DESK"

Once you have good people, naturally, you don't want to lose them. People need to feel secure at their place of employment, so they can focus on doing the job you're paying them for. You don't want them to worry that your company will start laying off or go out of business because you don't have enough work for them to do. You don't want them to spend their time looking for another job (or a second, additional job) in case this one doesn't work out. If you can alleviate—or eliminate—those worries, it helps people focus *not* on job-hunting but on doing the job they already have and doing it better.

After all, that's what "job security" is all about.

Our primary goal was to create strong job security at Mustang because it was important to improving productivity as well as longevity. Accordingly, we developed a system of overloading on work—not so much that people would feel overwhelmed, but just enough that they would feel secure. If they knew there was another project waiting for them when they finished the one they were working on, they were more likely to work harder to finish the current project. The "job on the corner of the desk" became our mantra, and our people were encouraged to "please hurry up and finish, so you can get onto this next project."

In addition to relieving the stress people had about possibly needing to find a new job, this philosophy increased efficiency. Many people find it difficult to finish projects if they don't have a firm deadline or if there's nothing waiting on the corner of their desk. As the old saying goes, "work expands to fill the time allotted," and projects tend to drag out unnecessarily. We didn't want that to happen—and you don't either, no matter what type of business or organization you're in. The promise of the next project helped people finish projects on time, and it even helped them to think of innovative ways to be *more* efficient and to push to complete the projects they were working on. All so that they could get to the next hot project—the "shiny object" on their desk that attracted them.

This approach was in stark contrast to what had traditionally happened in our industry—and in many other industries that operate in boom-and-bust cycles. If there's not another project waiting in the wings, people get laid off. We had seen this happen too many times, and I'm sure you have, too. That's not good business: not for you, not for your organization, and not for your employees. Nobody wins when that happens.

An added benefit of the job on the corner of the desk (or your equivalent for keeping people secure in their role with enough work) ties in to retaining great people. ***When people work together longer, they develop efficiencies and work faster and more productively.*** That efficiency reduced the labor hours required to do a project, which made our cost per project competitive even at fully loaded labor-billing rates. Therefore, we could pay the most competitive rate for people and still have a lower estimated cost in our bids—a win for the person, for our client, and for the business!

In contrast, when you have new people joining your organization all the time, they need to come up to speed, which slows down business. That speed, which is tied to tenured people, creates a competitive advantage for you, against other companies.

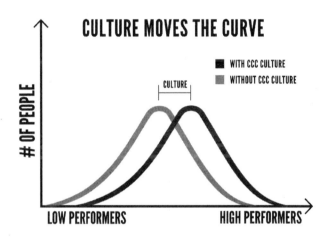

CULTURE MOVES THE CURVE

■ WITH CCC CULTURE
■ WITHOUT CCC CULTURE

CULTURE

OF PEOPLE

LOW PERFORMERS   HIGH PERFORMERS

Everyone pulls in the same bell-shaped curve of people no matter how good their hiring is. Our (and hopefully your) people are more efficient and stay longer, creating a difference in performance that pumps up the bottom line.

For example, one of our teams did the first Spar production platform in the world for Anadarko. A Spar is an innovative type of oil platform used in very deep waters of 3,000 to 7,000 feet. Our team needed to develop new technologies because of the nature of the floating structure. Later, people on that team worked together on the next Spar production platform, which reduced costs and schedules, because they didn't have to revisit decisions they had made on the previous project. We used elements of prior work, called "go-bys" for the new designs. Over time, that team continued to work together on eight Spar platforms without any hiccups. That's the beauty of continuity: greater efficiency with predictable results and more profit for the client, the vendors, and us ... Making Heroes!

Finally, the job on the corner of the desk also meant that there wasn't as much downtime in our overhead costs. This led to increased profitability within the standard billing rates for our industry. This efficiency was where we were able to squeeze out bonus money for everyone who was working so hard. In short, the job on the corner of the desk approach to work forced a sales discipline and a completion discipline. **Sales had to close and projects had to close.**

ACQUIRING PEOPLE FROM ANOTHER COMPANY WITHOUT ACQUIRING THE COMPANY

We also acquired entire companies of people without acquiring the companies themselves. These were called "no-cost acquisitions." Instead of buying a company and working to trim out the "corporate fat" while fighting the inertia of the acquired business, we left the fat behind.

Distressed companies, or parts of companies, or key-management team members were identified and then offered a solution. We were able to put their people to work on our projects, while the overhead people closed down their business unit or moved into other areas of their company.

Another strategy was to hire full management teams from other companies and let them bring in people or teams from their previous employers or contacts. This way, they redeveloped their capability under a much leaner and more responsive leadership team at our company. For example, during our first year in business, Dave Rucker merged his engineering firm into our company, and that "merger" brought us some good technical computer programs and raised our profile with industry leaders who had great respect for Dave. They helped spread the word that he was now with Mustang.

A few years later, we did it again. We essentially acquired most of Wilcrest Engineering at no cost. We received a call from Benton Oil & Gas managers asking if we could pick up the engineering team they had been working with at Wilcrest. Wilcrest was suffering in a downturn, people were leaving the team and this was negatively impacting their project. This was Operation Horsethief on steroids: the entire team that worked at Wilcrest was moved to Mustang without actually buying their company! Essentially, we just picked up their payroll and the project.

This happened again in the eighth year. A company called Litwin had recently been acquired by Raytheon Engineers & Constructors. We weren't familiar with Litwin, but an executive recruiter we respected called and told us about the company. At one time, Litwin had 1,500 engineers doing refinery and petrochemical projects, but it had shrunk to 750 by the time of the acquisition due to one of the industry downturns. When Raytheon bought Litwin, it offered six-month contracts to Litwin's key managers to ensure continuity. However, Raytheon made so many changes in the first three months, people who hadn't signed contracts started being snapped up by competing companies.

Litwin had been a very stable company: many of its engineers and support staff had worked there for fifteen to thirty years—which was impressive and a lot like our company. It had a good people oriented culture that would match well with ours. Moreover, Litwin had expertise in refinery and petrochemical, an area we wanted to get into for diversification. So, Mustang hired the leadership team when their contracts expired and, over the next fifteen months, continued to cherry-pick those whom we felt were the company's best 300 engineers and support people. They had either left or had put their resumes on the street, so we weren't raiding these other firms; these people were already looking for new jobs. They were happy to rejoin their old team, which was now at Mustang.

Most people would think that the Raytheon senior managers would be angry about our hiring some of their best people. But Raytheon was such a big company that its managers in this area had the "People … they're replaceable" attitude. Hiring all those teams, with all that experience—especially in the specific area we wanted to get into—made our company a major player in that space within two years, a feat that would likely have taken eight years to develop brick-by-brick organically.

GREAT COMPANIES ATTRACT GREAT PEOPLE

One of the best benefits of building a people-oriented company with a strong team culture is that eventually, you don't have to look for great employees; they'll find *you.*

An amazing example of this happened to us in our fifth year. David Edgar, the senior vice president of engineering at a 100-year-old pipeline company called us. One of our company's cofounders, Felix, had worked with David there—which is obviously another example of how important it is to keep in touch with people you used to work with. Anyway, David wanted to grow his operation; he was based in Louisiana, and he felt he needed a presence in Houston, where many projects originated. Stunningly, we learned that the real reason for his call was that he wanted to buy part of our company—

or perhaps the entire company! However flattering, we weren't interested in selling to a larger company at that time.

A year later, David Edgar came back with another buyout offer, but our company had doubled in size, and we still weren't interested in selling. David was so impressed by our growth and people-oriented leadership that he quit his job and came to work for us! He decided to build a Houston pipeline group within Mustang and leave his previous company. In short, we had effected a "reverse acquisition," and it cost us only David Edgar's salary—an investment that was well worth it! Mustang was a major player in the pipeline industry within four years.

That's what can happen when you keep in touch with former colleagues and build an organization that they want to work for: you attract the best and the brightest. Don't overlook that in your own organization: think about all the people you've met and worked with who might bring something valuable to where you are now. You can build a superteam and leave your competitors in the dust.

"GENETIC TESTING" OF NEW HIRES

I talk more about organizational structure in chapter 4, but before then, I want to make an important point about how the structure and nature of a company affects how you hire. Or, more specifically, *whom* you hire to fit the company values and culture.

From the very beginning of our company, we were incredibly flexible. We did a wide variety of projects for a huge number of clients that necessitated moving our people to wherever they were needed or would add the most value. Therefore, people we hired needed to also be very flexible. We called this "genetic testing," as we were looking for what we called "Mustang DNA" in new hires. It was *critical* to bring on board people who could adjust to constantly changing projects, market conditions, even locations—because about a third of our people would follow projects out to the field to support construction work.

WE WERE LOOKING FOR WHAT WE CALLED "MUSTANG DNA" IN NEW HIRES. IT WAS *CRITICAL* TO BRING ON BOARD PEOPLE WHO COULD ADJUST TO CONSTANTLY CHANGING PROJECTS, MARKET CONDITIONS, EVEN LOCATIONS.

If the people we interviewed had "Mustang DNA," then they would feel completely at home in our company, which was totally project-oriented and client-focused. Those people wouldn't care how big their office was or if they even had an office or who they reported to or what their title was. None of that mattered to us, and if it didn't matter to people who were considering working for our company, then they would be a good fit. They would understand Making Heroes. The people we brought on board had the same priorities we did: they wanted to get the job done, work with a tight-knit team, and do a great job that would impress their clients. They knew that those clients would hire Mustang again, which created terrific job security for everyone.

We progressed from doing $20 million simple projects in 100 feet of water to doing $5 billion "floating cities" in 8,000 feet of water in eight years! The deep-water projects required "space-age" technologies and 1,000-person teams. Those projects required tremendous flexibility in our people in order to grow with such a rapidly evolving industry.

Whatever your values are, you want to make sure the new people you hire *share* those values. If they don't, those people won't last long, and you'll be looking to fill that same position all too soon. Don't look past a poor attitude or not working well with others in order to get someone's expertise. They have to come in with your DNA as you do not have the time to try and develop it in someone.

Having the right DNA will build better teams and help insure repeat work from clients.

HIRE YOUNG PEOPLE TO KEEP YOUR BUSINESS CURRENT

Many organizations focus on hiring people with five-plus years of experience, because those new employees will be able to come up to speed more quickly. That's true—and if you're hiring people using the suggestions I've provided so far in this chapter, you may be doing this, too. We certainly did. Since my cofounders and I were all in our thirties when we started our business, the people we knew and hired were primarily our age or older.

But don't discount the "kids" who are fresh out of school—or even still in school. We learned this lesson after hiring our first intern, Kristen Peterson, a mechanical-engineering major who had just completed her sophomore year in college. She had good computer skills, so we assigned her to the design room, figuring that when she went back to school in the fall, she could show her professors and fellow students some drawings she created over the summer.

Little did we know how much she would teach *us!* Because she was computer savvy, she watched what the designers were doing, and then she figured out how to do those tasks more efficiently using tools in the computer-aided design (CAD) software. She challenged our people daily. By the third week of her internship, we had fifteen-year veterans with three years of CAD experience raving about her because she had shown them shortcuts they could take in their design work.

Kristen showed us that we needed to figure out how to bring new graduates into our company. Our industry had already gone ten years without bringing in any young people, because clients didn't want anyone with minimal experience working on their projects. We understood that viewpoint, but we also realized it was short-sighted, because eventually there would be a severe age gap in training future leaders. So, we started the "Young Guns (YG)" program, where we hired recent college and high school graduates each year. Every YG with ten-plus years of experience was in a leadership position by 2016. They were technical leads, department managers, and in corporate leadership ... truly homegrown talent.

RETAINING GOOD PEOPLE BY COMMUNICATING MORE AND BETTER

It's not enough to hire the best people, train them well, and develop an organizational culture where they'll want to come to work and do a great job. To have the kind of low turnover that we had—remember, it was less than 5 percent, compared to the 35 percent in most of our industry—it's critical to *retain* your people.

How do you do that? *Communicate.* This was a lesson for me as a combat engineer company commander in the US Army. We had gone to an all-volunteer force, and we were having trouble getting soldiers to reenlist before their terms of service expired. The army provided a card system that reminded me to talk with each person once a quarter, one-on-one, wherever I bumped into them—in the motor pool or out in the field on maneuvers. We talked about their interests and how to get them engaged in those activities. Once these soldiers felt that they were being valued and listened to, there was no trouble in meeting reenlistment targets. In fact, I felt comfortable not offering reenlistment to low performers. Making communication with my individual soldiers a daily priority helped build a strong unit.

Similarly, at Mustang we pushed communication with our employees from the beginning.

Not long after starting Mustang, we brought in David Sneed, a lead piping designer from a well-respected medium-size firm that was closing down. He came in initially as a contract employee (in keeping with our low-overhead approach in the early years), yet we could see that he was a top talent who would have no problem with the hectic pace of our company.

Shortly after David joined us, Mustang was hired to do a project with a tight budget that would require us to be very creative. The project manager needed to streamline the number of labor hours, so he sketched out all the piping and turned the plans over to design, with directions to "not change anything; just input it." He did this with the best of intentions, as he wanted to take care of the client and stay within the client's budget. However, these instructions upset David, who felt that if this was the way our company worked, someone with his abilities wouldn't be needed. He didn't want or need to be spoon-fed piping design solutions drawn by an engineer, so he told the project manager he was going to quit.

Of course, that wasn't what the project manager had intended, and he tried to explain to David why he had given those instructions. When that failed to dissuade David from leaving, the project manager asked me and my partner Felix to talk with him. We didn't say anything different from what the project manager had said, but the fact that all of us were willing and eager to talk with him to persuade him to stay was compelling.

What we had here, as the old saying goes, was "a failure to communicate." I explained to David how much our company *values* designers, and how we believed that design is the backbone of an engineering office. In fact, engineers get much of their real-world training from designers, before they move into coordination and management of projects. Designers are critical to creating the consistency and reputation of the firm, because the success of a project is determined by how easy it is to build from the drawings that go out the door.

David was also told that part of our vision was to raise design up to a more respected and professional level. We wanted to hold on to good designers just as much as good engineers. As mentioned earlier, our philosophy was that people weren't "a dime a dozen" or that they were easy to replace. Fortunately, David listened and believed in our values and philosophy and hired on as a full-time employee. Later the same year, he took over as the lead of the piping design group. He was a rock that we built on, and he stayed with the company until he retired, twenty-seven years later.

That's the kind of longevity every organization wants!

KEEP TRACK OF TALENT IN YOUR INDUSTRY

If you follow all the advice and suggestions offered in this chapter, you may find there are too *many* good people you could hire. What a great problem to have! That was a problem we had, too, but a smart solution was found to solve it: *keep track of them.*

Sometime around our fourth year, we created a simple "talent directory" of all the technical expertise available in Houston that might be needed in the future. Houston was the center of the oil and gas industry, so every skill required for any project in the world was available. Companies just needed to be able to tap into people with that skill set when needed, instead of carrying them on their payroll. Some of these experts were hired full time, but only when the volume of work in a particular area increased to where their abilities were needed.

Our directory eventually grew to twenty-eight categories of expertise, with a wide variety, from compressor vibration to naval architecture. To further feed the directory, we encouraged all of our department managers to contribute to these lists as they found great resources. Having this tool at our fingertips gave us the confidence that we could work on many different types of projects, in all areas of our industry.

Another good idea is to keep people in mind to hire later if you're not able to hire them initially. For example, Craig Devenney was working for one of our clients when he approached us and said he'd like to work at Mustang. However, he couldn't come on board right then as he wanted to finish the project he was on and not leave his employer high and dry. Craig had a breadth of experience in engineering, project management, and construction, so we knew he would be able to help us immensely. After working out an offer that he agreed to, it was put in a drawer until he was ready to change jobs. A year later, he came, and he stayed for fifteen years!

Don't let good people slip away. Talent is *not easily* replaceable. Good people are hard to find. Once you've found them, keep them in mind, even if you're not ready or able to hire them when you first meet them. Ask everyone in your organization to add to the talent directory, and then use it when you need it.

Continuously ask everyone in your organization to be recruiting for you in a variety of ways, in good times and bad. This will ensure that you have top-quality individuals to choose from. ***Quality comes through choice.***

OBJECTIVE:

Break the code on hiring and retaining people with your "success" DNA to become a Culture Code Champion. The reduced hiring and training costs and increased efficiency will make your people happier and will boost your bottom line.

HIRE RIGHT: CONTINUOUSLY RECRUIT TOP TALENT

KEY POINTS TO KEEP IN MIND ABOUT HIRING RIGHT:

1. Great employees are not "a dime a dozen." When you find talented, hard-working people, *do everything you can to keep them. Don't let skilled workers slip away. You can drive your annual turnover to less than 5 percent and pump up your bottom line.*

2. What's your culture costing you? *Visit CultureCodeChampions.com and fill out the Culture Code Champions Culture Assessment. Print it out to take notes on as you read this book. Also complete the Culture Cost Calculator to predict the dollar savings to your bottom line. These tools provide you with a method and a goal for building a culture of champions.*

3. Good people know other good people, so why look outside when you don't have to? *Referral hiring is easier, less expensive, and builds a stronger organization. Labeling it "Operation Horsethief" or being a "talent magnet" is a fun way to keep people always looking for strong players.*

4. You can train job-placement agencies to identify the type of people you want, *and they will call you when they find good applicants. Let them be your part-time HR group to sort through prospects.*

5. The "job on the corner of the desk" motivates people to finish what they're doing *so they can move on to something new. It forces a sales discipline and a completion discipline. Both sales and projects have to close.*

6. Look for "no-cost acquisitions," where you can hire entire teams of people *from a company that's closing or struggling, without actually having to acquire the whole company. Leave the "corporate fat" behind.*

7. Build a great people-oriented company, *and you won't have to search for great employees; they'll find you.*

8. Hire people who are flexible and adaptable to changing projects and market conditions. *Make sure they share your organization's values from the get-go. Check that potential new people share your company's "DNA" to ensure a good fit.*

9. Develop your own "Young Guns" program, because young people literally are our future. *Although they don't have the experience that your seasoned people do, they bring a wealth of knowledge about new technology that we can all learn from. They also bring fresh eyes and energy that can invigorate your culture and keep your longer-term people on their toes.*

10. Make sure your employees know they're respected and valued. *That's the real key to a successful organization and staff longevity. Communicate honestly with your people regularly. It works in the army for reenlistment, and it will work for you.*

11. Keep track of great people even if you can't hire them now. *You will know where they are when you need them. A "talent directory" is a resource every organization should have and keep up to date.*

12. Continuous recruiting in good times and bad must become a habit to create the culture you want. *Talent attracts talent!*

Note: Following is a worksheet that is provided at the end of each chapter. It identifies which of the 7 Culture Code Champion Steps we want you to evaluate in a SWOT (strength, weakness, opportunity, threat) analysis.

Then, we want you to identify your Champion for implementing that step and turning it into a long term habit. Pick a "buddy" from another area to foster cross-fertilization. They will hold each other accountable for implementing the initial plan and developing it into a habit.

Fashion a baton (or purchase them from Culture Code Champions) and have a ceremony for handing it to the Champion to put in their area.

This two person team will implement and report against the agreed KPIs (key performance indicators) for that culture step.

CULTURE CODE CHAMPIONS WORKSHEET: STEP 6: CONTINUOUSLY RECRUIT TOP TALENT

STRENGTH:
Internal:_____
_____

WEAKNESS:
Internal:_____
_____

OPPORTUNITY:
External:_____
_____

THREAT:
External:_____
_____

CHAMPION:
Hand Step 6 baton to: _____
    Buddy: _____
Conceptual initial actions:
    1._____
    2._____
    3._____
    4._____
Start Date: _____

CHAPTER 2

CRAFT YOUR CULTURE: CREATE A SENSE OF TEAM

O nce you've hired outstanding people, do everything you can think of to keep them. The longer your people work together, the more efficient, productive, and happy they'll be—which in turn will enable your company to survive and thrive. My cofounders and I had worked for other companies that did not have an open, inclusive culture, and we truly wanted to build a different and better organization. We wanted to create a culture where we had the hearts and minds of our people, so we motivated them by building strong teams and an internal brand.

I learned a lot about culture during my senior year at West Point while taking a leadership class based on a book by management guru Peter Drucker, and I leaned heavily on that as a company commander in the US Army. One idea that is generally attributed to Drucker is

"Culture eats strategy for breakfast." That doesn't mean your organization's strategy *isn't* important to your success, just that *culture* is much *more* important.

We took that credo to heart when founding our brand, Mustang. This chapter describes what we did, and I trust it will give you some building blocks for what you can do in your company or organization. It worked for us as we grew our business to a billion dollars, (which is tough to do, even in the oil and gas industry). I firmly believe it can work for any organization willing to commit to changing its culture. Here are some ideas.

YOUR COMPANY NAME IS MORE IMPORTANT THAN YOU THINK

Even before Paul, Felix, and I started our company, we believed that building a strong brand—one that would be immediately identifiable to the outside world—was just as important as building a strong culture for our business. Our brand would be constantly felt *inside* our organization as well as outside. That's one of the reasons we debated long and hard before choosing our company name.

That may sound like a small decision to some of you. You may be thinking, *What's in a name? Just pick something and get business cards printed.* But we thought the name of our company was *very* important.

Many companies use their owners' initials to create their name: for example, our former company had done this: they called their firm CBS Engineering. We decided not to do that, because we wanted our company to be able to grow beyond just the three of us. We thought of ourselves more as caretakers than owners ... think about that.

After considering lots of options, we finally settled on a name—

but then learned that another company had already registered it in Texas. So, it was back to the drawing board.

Ideas can come from the wildest of places, if you're open-minded enough to brainstorm. Our company name was inspired by my wife, in fact, who didn't even work in the company—she was a registered nurse, working full time. One day on her way to work, she was stuck in traffic, so she started writing down the names of some of the cars she saw. She figured that car manufacturers invest a lot of money in naming their products so that they'll have broad appeal, and she thought maybe we could benefit from their research.

While looking at her list of twelve names, Mustang jumped out at us. It was easy to spell and understand worldwide, and it generally invoked positive thoughts in people. The Mustang is an iconic car— one that changed the automotive industry, under the legendary leadership of Lee Iacocca. In fact, the Mustang car propelled his rise to the top of Ford Motor Company—real horsepower there! Plus, the energy, strength, and stamina of Mustang horses were things we could be passionate about.

Of course, I realize that many of you reading this book are working for companies or organizations that already have a name— and there's nothing you can do about it. That doesn't mean you can't pick a name for *your* particular team or group or department or division—something that your people can rally around.

For example, my son grew up seeing and feeling what we called the "Mustang Motion," how it operated, and the unbelievable loyalty it created. He named his company "Fab Fours," because he made parts for four-wheel-drive vehicles. But he could not come up with an identity from that name.

Over time, he worked his vision and values with his people and they decided to declare themselves "pirates." They planned to "attack" their market, take over the truck and jeep bumper industry, and share the "bounty."

Whenever he is speaking to his people and raises his fist, they all yell "Aaaarrrggghhh!" You can tell that they cannot wait for him to do it! At times, he even dresses up as a pirate to stir up enthusiasm. Fab Fours is producing 50 percent more product per person than its competition due to the company's team culture and homegrown lean-manufacturing methods. It is the leading American bumper manufacturer in terms of both quality and on-time delivery.

It's what you *do* to leverage that name that will help you with branding inside your organization and with external perception. That leads us to the next aspect of culture that's so important …

DEVELOP A SPIRIT OF *BELONGING*

People want to *belong* to something—that's why sports fans buy jerseys with the number of their favorite player, as well as jackets, hats, banners, and blankets from their favorite teams. It's why people buy bumper stickers supporting their favorite causes and why they put political signs on their front lawns. They want to belong, and they want to *show* they belong to something they are passionate about.

For some reason, though, this sense of belonging very rarely happens where people work. In reality, most of us spend a significant amount of our lives at work—at least eight hours a day, and in many companies, even more hours than that. So why isn't there more of a team mentality at work? Here is an example of how we bonded teams together in the army.

• • •

The second platoon I led in the army was the Atomic Demolitions platoon of the First Cavalry Division. There was only one "nuke platoon" per division, so I reported directly through my battalion commander to the division commander, a general officer. We knew we were "special," because everyone was hand-picked for such things as education, dexterity, and a solid background, as identified by a top secret clearance review. We were a tight-knit team that worked together in a secure facility every day.

One time, the battalion operations officer tasked us with running a Survival Escape Resistance and Evasion (SERE) course for the battalion, which entailed four days of specialized training for each of six companies. This was a big challenge for my platoon of twenty-eight people, but the battalion operations officer knew we had top caliber soldiers. The first three days consisted of skills training on escape, evasion, orienteering, living off the land, and resistance to interrogation.

In order to make the training very realistic, we requested that some of the division's aviation, infantry and military police units be put under our control for the "evasion night." This last night culminated in a company conducting an air assault of a hill, being overrun by my "enemy" platoon, then using their new SERE skills to get to a rally point eight miles away. We coordinated the helicopters, infantry-unit listening points to help capture soldiers, and a military police POW camp with interrogators, as well as possible methods of escaping. It was good cross-training for a number of units across the division and was a ton of fun for my guys. I loved the experience of running a hand-picked team of people who had pride in their work and strong camaraderie. The SERE training loosened them up before they later had to knuckle down and pass the annual National Surety Inspection to certify the division's nuclear capability.

The army did everything possible to get soldiers involved and proud of their units. There were patches, flags, songs, history, myths, and lore. It was even more pronounced in Ranger and Delta Force units—where many of my West Point classmates excelled. When things got tough on the battlefield, we wanted our troops to take care of each other and work as a well-honed team. A sense of belonging was critical. This was emphasized in the *Black Hawk Down* story in the preface of this book.

• • •

From the very first days of Mustang, we wanted our people to feel they belonged to something different. So, all our employees were called "Mustangers," and we found that referring to ourselves by that fun name had a huge impact. It felt like we were all members of a club that other people should want to be a part of. And it didn't stop there. Like in the army, there were mottos, myths, a hand sign, a song, a banner, a mascot, and many traditions.

We also branded the Mustang name and horse logo on all sorts of useful objects we gave to our people. In many companies, this stuff we all get (swag) is only given to clients, but we wanted to be different. Having worked at companies where the clients regularly got baseball hats and other items, but the employees never did, we knew that didn't instill much of a sense of belonging or loyalty. That may sound like a petty complaint, but it's the little things that many people notice and remember.

The cost savings in getting people to stay three to five years instead of one makes the cost of these morale builders insignificant. Our goal was to have people think, "If it is Mustang, it is fun and energetic." Plus, these "goodies" were tangible evidence of our appreciation for everyone's efforts.

We didn't give out Mustang merchandise at certain times or only to certain people. Instead, new things were continually introduced and left on people's desks, randomly, throughout the year. Special swag was also provided to company, project, and family team-building activities. It was an easy way to keep people energized and talking positively about their team. This can work in any organization. Energizing people, however, is like piling sand: you have to keep at it.

Giving to our people was part of internal sales: treat your people like you treat your clients, and they will notice!

In fact, Mustangers still maintain a Facebook page that shows swag they have collected over the years. Even though some of them don't work for the company anymore, they *still* identify as "Mustangers," due to the life-changing experiences there.

BUILDING TEAM SPIRIT BY HAVING FUN OUTSIDE OF WORK

Another aspect of culture that's critical is team building. Entire books have been written on this subject, but I can speak only from my own experience. I was fortunate to have experienced terrific culture and team building in the Boy Scouts, at West Point, and in the army, due to the team spirit and camaraderie that each group engendered.

Unfortunately, after leaving the army, I worked at companies that had no spirit of teamwork at all. That's why my cofounders and I were so *determined* to create a company that would be nothing like anywhere we had worked before in the industry. Since you spend so much of your life at work, if you don't like your co-workers and you don't enjoy working with them, that's when you start not liking your job. You find yourself counting the days until you can either move on or retire.

We wanted to build strong teams that felt a sense of bonding to each other and to the company. One nice thing about team building is that you don't have to spend a fortune taking your people on fancy getaways, arranging meetings at vacation resorts, or hiring an outside firm to conduct "team building exercises" for you. All you need to do is make sure that everything you do with your people is *fun*.

OUR EFFORTS TO BUILD "TEAM SPIRIT" CREATED A CULTURE WHERE PEOPLE WANTED TO WORK HARDER, BETTER, AND TOGETHER—AND THEY DIDN'T WANT TO LEAVE OUR COMPANY.

Easier said than done? Not really. Good food and genuine interest in other people will go a long way. Dressing up in a costume or perhaps wearing a weird hat also helps break the ice. People cannot resist smiling and joining in on the fun if the leader or a client is opening him or herself up to be part of the high spirits and the team fun.

Before you roll your eyes and decide to skip to the next section of this book, you should know that our efforts to build "team spirit" created a culture where people wanted to work harder, better, and together—and they didn't want to leave our company.

So how did we build team spirit? The first "team-building exercise" Mustang did happened by chance. It was early days, and as mentioned, we were frugal. Our secondhand office bookcases were pretty cheap—a lesson learned the hard way when there was a loud crash in the office one day. One of our new hires was moving in and put his heavy vendor data manuals on one of our lightweight particle-board bookcases, which immediately collapsed. It occurred to me that there was an easy way to fix this problem: instead of buying another cheap bookshelf, I would build one.

That weekend, I built a bookshelf that would hold the weight of our heaviest manuals. That was easy … until we realized we needed about ten more exactly like that one. From my team building experiences in the Boy Scouts and the army, it seemed the best way to get many bookshelves built quickly was to treat the project like an old-fashioned barn raising. Anyone who was willing to join us was invited to my house the following weekend, where we would have lunch together and build bookshelves.

Apparently, the idea appealed to others at our company, too, because about fifteen people showed up ready and raring to work. I don't think it was because "the boss" had invited them, either: they said they came because it sounded like fun. Many of the people helping that weekend said they had done similar projects for schools, the Houston Rodeo, church camps, and Scouts, but no one had ever done anything like this for their company.

The shelves turned out great, but the real benefit of the day was that while working together; we *got to know each other as people*. Everyone talked about their families, their hobbies and talents outside of work, and other things they liked to do in their spare time. You don't often get the opportunity to have those types of conversations when you're on the job—hopefully, you're too busy working! This was a genuine bonding experience that gave everyone insight into each other's personal lives. And when you *really* get to know people, you can work better with them on all types of projects, and you can start tearing down the natural silos that build up in every organization. We called this activity providing "free space" for people, from top to bottom in the organization, to interact with no formal structure.

Because the bookshelf building day was fun and productive and led to better communication among our people, we decided to do whatever possible to extend this feeling of belonging. A month after

49

starting the company, everyone joined us for a picnic at a local lake. They brought their families and a potluck dish and enjoyed some sailing and water skiing together. A few months later, my partner Felix turned forty, and his wife threw him a birthday party at their house and invited the whole company. Everyone had a great time, and we even overheard someone say, "This is the first time I have ever been to a company owner's house." The positive feedback encouraged us to do more.

Paul's wife brought in a home-cooked lunch every Friday so all of us could eat together as a team. This ended (after two years!) when Kay had to brake suddenly on the way to our office, and lasagna spilled all over her back seat ... but by then, everyone was welded into a team!

Thanksgiving luncheons were held—to give thanks both for the work Mustang was getting and for the spirit of camaraderie in our people. There were only about twenty people our first year in business, so it was a small gathering held on-site. However, by our eighth year, we had 250 people come, and in our twentieth year, we had 2,500 Mustangers and their family members attend. Obviously, as the number of people attending grew, it wasn't possible to host these events in our offices, and we ultimately had to rent out space in the community.

Our Christmas parties were different from other companies' parties, too. One company I had worked for had no outside activities at all: everyone just worked eight hours a day and then went home. The company did host an end-of-year holiday party, in a banquet room at a local hotel. I'll never forget it: in the center of the room were two huge, circular tables, under spotlights, with a spread of great food. But since no one really knew each other well, there wasn't much interaction or mingling happening. Moreover, the mood was bleak because the industry was in a major downturn, the company had recently laid off people, and others had left on their own, because they thought the company was a sinking ship. As a result, the people who did attend the party stood against the walls of the room, in semi-darkness: no one wanted to go under the lights to get some of the food, almost as though they were afraid to call attention to themselves and become the next to get the axe. It was the most depressing Christmas party I had ever been to. I felt like maybe I should go back into the army, where all of our unit parties were fun, with a lot of camaraderie, joking, and storytelling.

In contrast, our first Mustang Christmas party was held at my house, where Paul, Felix, and I handed out a crisp new fifty-dollar bill to each of our employees, including our contract workers. We encouraged them to spend this money on something for themselves, because we knew how hard they worked to provide for their families. Many people—again, including contract workers—also received end-of-year bonus checks, to emphasize our intention to share Mustang's success with them.

No one could believe that cash and bonuses also went to contract employees, because our competitors treated their contract workers differently from their full-time employees. However, it was obvious that our contract people were working just as hard as our direct employees, and we wanted to show how much that work ethic was valued. Additionally, gifts (which had been wrapped by our very supportive wives) were handed out: golf shirts with the Mustang logo for Mustangers and Christmas tree ornaments for their spouses. As mentioned, the team spirit of Mustangers was reinforced as often as possible with hats, shirts, and countless other items.

Moreover, we didn't celebrate only the holidays; we had events outside of work throughout the year. We also sponsored events that supported charities like rebuilding homes or delivering items to needy families in our community. It became clear to us that once you get the flywheel spinning on creating camaraderie, you need to keep giving it a periodic push. In our first year in business, we held our first "shrimp boil," with about eighty Mustangers, clients, and vendors attending—and a Goodyear Blimp happened to fly over the festivities in what everyone took as a salute! The shrimp boil was a big hit, and we realized that our events would be a catalyst for getting clients and vendors together for some fun. The next year, 200 people attended; the fourth year, there were more than 500 people, and by year six, we had more than a thousand people. The shrimp boil turned into an annual event—and it wasn't the only one.

There were swim parties, bowling leagues, softball and basketball teams, tennis and golf tournaments, and putt-putt games (teams created golf holes down the hallways). Mustang held offshore fishing trips, river-rafting and canoeing expeditions, paintball games, paper airplane and Halloween-costume contests. Again, this was to provide and encourage "free space" for people to mingle, top to bottom, in the organization and also allow their families to experience the Mustang spirit.

As mentioned, our clients and vendors attended a number of events and sometimes they even dressed up in costumes for them. At the monthly report meetings, clients would wear the hat the team had selected for managers that day. Exxon, Conoco, Texaco, Elf Aquitaine, Mobil, and others wholeheartedly participated to help build team spirit and be part of the Mustang difference.

A favorite picture we have is of the BP Clair project team dressed in Nordic attire for our annual chili cook-off. Clair was the first application of a Gulf of Mexico offshore platform design in the North Sea. The project went through conceptual design and pricing in the UK, then was brought to us to reduce the cost. The BP project engineer in the picture is wearing a floor mop for hair, with a bucket on top to look like a Norseman. (It actually looks better than I can describe.) When I congratulated him for his participation, he said, "I'd wear this on my head an entire year for the $300 million your team saved us on this project!" That was pretty awesome, considering that our engineering and management fee was less than $20 million … got to love a happy client having fun!

Again, you don't need to spend a lot of money to have fun times with your people; just spend what makes sense. Your people will enjoy doing an activity and appreciate those who put it together. For those of you wondering how all these events were planned, it's not as difficult as you might think. In the early days, when our company was still small, we did it all ourselves. But as the number of our employees increased, so did the number of "rabble-rousers," which is what we nicknamed our people who wanted to get involved and help plan events.

Our rabble-rousers were self-appointed: they took it upon themselves to make things happen, because they knew it would be fun, put a smile on people's faces, and create lasting memories. These are hallmarks of people who are passionate about something. We wanted that passion people have outside of work to be brought into the team. These activities also energized our young people and gave them great content to post on social media. People organized around their own interests; all they needed to do was start something, and it took on a life of its own! After a few years, marketing would meet with the rabble-rousers in December, plan events for the next year, and get funding approved.

By the way, we didn't need to worry that our rabble-rousers would spend more time planning parties and fun events than working, because everyone in the organization was accountable for meeting certain quarterly goals. In addition, everyone filled out time sheets with details on how they allocated their time to different projects. When I say "everyone," I mean it: everyone in the company, including me and my cofounders and from the top managers down turned in regular time sheets. Everyone was accountable for doing his or her work. When we first instituted this policy, there were some complainers, but it was made clear that if you didn't turn in a time sheet, you didn't get paid. That solved the problem very quickly! Our entire management team believed that if you could measure it, you could improve it. Time sheets provided the measurement and transparency needed throughout the company.

We also had people who told their supervisor they would rather have more money in their paycheck than have activities. Supervisors let them know that these activities were important to building our tight team culture by saying, "If you do not want to participate, we may not be the right company for you."

Your objective should be to have everyone participate and have fun. The events you plan don't need to cost a lot of money, and they don't need to take a lot of time to organize, especially if you have lots of people helping. The rewards you'll see are incredibly worthwhile.

ORGANIZATIONAL CULTURE CAN TRANSLATE TO OTHER COUNTRIES

Many organizations worry that their culture is homegrown and won't translate to other countries (or even regions of the same country!), if or when they start expanding beyond their home base. That thought crossed our minds, too, and some of the people in our Houston office said they didn't think Mustang could convey its culture once new offices were opened around the world.

From 2005 through 2014, Mustang opened several international offices that totaled about 2,500 people. Our first international office was in Woking, England, about thirty miles southwest of London, and it grew to about 450 people. Applying what we learned in Woking, we then opened offices in Perth, Australia (200 people), and in Melbourne (100 people). A few years later, our Mumbai, India, office opened, with about twenty-five hugely enthusiastic people. Later, we added about 300 people in Kuala Lumpur, Malaysia; another 300 in Bogota, Colombia; 800 as a result of a joint venture in Al-Khobar, Saudi Arabia; and about 250 people in Norway.

That's a lot of different cultures around the world, but as our marketing people liked to say, "There are Mustangers *everywhere*; they just don't know it yet!" There are people in every corner of the world who want to serve others, do high-quality work, collaborate closely with others, and have fun while doing it. Where they live or where they're from has nothing to do with those traits; they come from the person's *character*, not his or her nationality.

We strove to impart to all these international offices what our organization's culture meant to us. And they embraced it! For example, one of the events held every year was a Christmas-tree decorating contest, and one year, the Mumbai office won. There were only a small number of people working in that office, and even though almost 80 percent of the country is Hindu, 14 percent adheres to Islam, and only 2 percent is Christian, the religions of the people working in that office didn't matter. What mattered was that the tree-decorating contest was an important, fun event for the entire company, and the people in the Mumbai office gave it their all.

As I mentioned in the introduction, in 2016, the marketing group produced a short video where they asked people in the various international offices and the larger offices in America, "What does it mean to be a Mustanger?" Each person answered in his or her own language, and there were subtitles in English. Paul, Felix, and I were humbled by the words and phrases these people used: they were the same ones we had created during our first four years. The video ends with our horse mascot, "Blue," providing its thoughts, using sign language! This was *ten years* after the founders had retired from Mustang's day to day operations.

You *can* break down barriers that some think separate people in different parts of the world. Respect their local cultures, but invite them to belong to yours as well.

INSTILLING CULTURE FROM DAY ONE: NEW HIRE BREAKFASTS

Of course, work can't be all fun and games, or you won't have a business to run. So, let's get back to the main subject of this book, which is how to build a better business through building a team culture.

One practice managers advocated was getting people working on their team as soon as they started. This may sound very basic, but I've seen businesses (and other organizations) that bring in new employees and then basically ignore them until they need them to do something. There is a reason 70 percent of new hires don't make it to 12 months … and 60 percent don't even make it six months!

Our managers needed people to be productive *immediately*, so it never occurred to us to do that. Instead, new hires came in at seven o'clock in the morning on their first day, and they were working on projects by nine thirty. They were in an office, they had their computers, they were given a project and a goody bag of swag, they had met their project team, and they were billable. No one had ever seen a company operate like that, and it impressed them enormously. They could feel the positive energy in the hallways with each person they met.

It was like a big church where new members are connected as soon as possible to smaller groups, such as a Sunday-school class or the choir, so they feel the touches from other people and feel like they belong. They are not just a face in the crowd of thousands but are recognized as an individual, and personal bonds are formed early.

By the time Mustang had been in business for about ten years, we were growing so fast and bringing in so many new people every month that we needed a more organized way to bring new employees up to speed quickly on our culture. There were about 800 people working in the company at that time, and about twenty new hires were coming in each month.

Full disclosure: I appropriated this next idea from the CEO of Tivenca, an engineering firm in Caracas, Venezuela that was interested in linking up with a Houston firm. The CEO was impressed by our company culture, so we were talking about how to win the hearts and minds of people. He said he had discovered an oh-so-simple way to bring people on board from the outset.

What did he do? Once a month, he invited all the new people to a lunch prepared by his chef in the boardroom. (Many South American CEOs have huge offices and conference rooms, with a personal chef and servers for when they entertain clients and vendors.) Then he encouraged everyone to talk informally about their previous jobs, their experience, their outside interests or hobbies, and what they hoped to find in their new job. And as the conversations unfolded, he found opportunities to interject information about his company and its culture and values.

What a *great* idea that was! Most new hires had never been in a boardroom or had ever talked to a CEO before. They were flattered to be invited, and they were impressed with the welcoming attitude from the top person. That first lunch made them more receptive to understanding the company culture, and they wanted to become a part of it. Also, they shared their impression of that experience with their families, friends, and neighbors—thus acting as ambassadors for their new company.

Then and there, I realized this was *exactly* what our company should do. Our growth had us concerned that our culture would become watered down to the point where we might become "just another services firm in Houston." We didn't want *that* to happen!

We decided to invite all our new hires to breakfast, on the first Tuesday of the month (because Mondays are always hectic). We picked breakfast instead of lunch so that our people would come *before* going to the office. It is often difficult to break away from work in the middle of the day, so that excuse was eliminated.

We elaborated on the original idea by having our new employees meet not only the CEO—in our case, it was the three co-founders—but also managers from throughout the company. There would be a few managers at each table to get some cross-fertilization between veterans and new people.

Finally, the breakfasts were held at a nearby country club: for two reasons. First, holding them offsite made them more special than having breakfast in a break room or cafeteria (since we didn't have a fancy boardroom). Secondly, it occurred to us that many of the new hires might never have been to a country club before and would welcome the invitation. The breakfasts were buffet style, in an elegant room overlooking the golf course and full of white-tablecloth-covered tables.

These breakfasts were a great opportunity for new people to see our organization's culture in action from the get-go. The managers who attended talked about projects they had worked on that they were proud of, about current projects and how Mustang had won them, and about upcoming projects they were excited about. The managers also talked about people who had moved from one area of the company to another, which was important to show that they believed in cross-training, flexibility, and individual growth across our organization.

The managers were clearly very comfortable with each other, so there was a strong feeling of familiarity and friendship in the room. It was obvious how tightly knit our people were, how much energy there was about our projects, the dedication to quality that everyone talked about, and the communication seen across disciplines.

People felt personal job security from seeing the breadth and depth of the company talent gathered in the room. They were also impressed that the owners felt this activity was important enough to attend and participate in.

Our new people were all invited to tell the group something about themselves: what companies they came from, what departments they were working in at Mustang, and what specific projects they were working on—because, as described above, our new employees were assigned projects on day one. And, of course they were also encouraged to refer outstanding people they had worked with—thereby introducing them to Operation Horsethief!

At the end of the breakfast, the new people were thanked again by everyone for choosing Mustang. They were given a goody bag with company swag for them and their families, a printed Power-Point handout, and our *Newsy Newsletter*. We didn't use PowerPoint during the breakfast, but we did want them to have something they could look at later (and share with their spouses) that described Mustang, our culture, and an overview of our core philosophies. The *Newsy Newsletter* was always snail-mailed home to engage the spouses and children. Hard-copy communication was important in keeping families informed.

This was such a simple thing to do, yet it was very effective and important to our organization's culture. I encourage everyone I meet to do something similar in their own organizations, because I truly believe these "getting-to-know-you" meals are an easy way to welcome new people and get them excited about the new positions they've just undertaken. For anyone who has sat through the mind-numbingly boring presentations about HR policies during their first days of work, these breakfasts are a feel-good and successful change of pace.

And for those skeptics out there who think they can't afford the time or money to do this, no time was lost because the breakfasts happened *before* the start of the workday. And you can spend whatever you can afford: if you can't afford to host a breakfast for new employees once a month, you can certainly afford fruit and pastry platters and some coffee, and you'll achieve essentially the same result. It's not about the food; it's about the *interaction* between the managers and the new hires/employees. Trust me: your new people will be impressed, and they'll come up to speed more quickly because they'll be enthusiastic about the organization they've just joined.

REVIEW PERFORMANCE AND REWARD PEOPLE *REGULARLY AND OFTEN*

Because Mustang started as a three-person company, there wasn't a lot of the bureaucracy that you typically find in larger, more-established companies. We added people, but we tried not to add any systems that might distract us from getting work done, taking care of our clients, and taking care of our people. One thing we didn't have was annual performance reviews. Even later, as the company expanded in size, such formalized processes were never added.

You might think that wrought havoc among our employees, but nothing could be further from the truth. That's because instead of sitting down once a year to have a short meeting with a supervisor or manager, **everyone knew *at all times* how they were doing.** Managers made a point of telling them often.

Each department manager had a simple matrix with the names of all the people in that department listed in the left-hand column and the months of the year across the top. Managers were encouraged to talk to every one of their people every month in the hallway or after a meeting … just visiting with them on what they were doing well and anything they needed to do. So, their "reviews" were continuous and based on ongoing performance.

This also encouraged managers to get out of their offices and interact with people. Management By Wandering Around (MBWA) was critical to culture and leadership development.

Continuous reviews are a much better way to manage people. Anyone who has ever had to conduct a performance review knows how difficult it is to recall *everything* the person they're reviewing has done over an entire year, and everyone risks reviewing people only on the basis of what they've done recently. Our system of monthly conversations eliminated that problem by simply giving into it: managers *were* reviewing people on what they had done lately. That enabled them to give immediate positive feedback to people who had done a great job on a project; it also enabled managers to help or counsel employees who weren't performing as well as they hoped or expected. Who wants to wait an entire year to do that?

Also, instead of everyone waiting for an annual review and a hoped-for pay increase, managers gave out bonuses *whenever someone did an impressive job.* I know that sounds radical to most people who work in traditional companies, where bonuses are given out either at the end of the calendar year or after the end of the fiscal year. In some cases, that is done simply to hold onto people those extra few months, because managers don't trust their ability to retain talented individuals in their company. But just like annual performance reviews, that practice seemed counter-productive to us. People staying to get a bonus will not perform to the highest standard; they are already thinking about their next job. People should be rewarded *when they perform well,* not a year later!

Moreover, this practice is not difficult to implement. At the beginning of each year, each department manager was given a set amount they could give as bonuses for each person in their department; the managers were then free to give out bonuses from that total, anytime during the year that they thought it was appropriate.

Employees appreciated that "instant gratification" so much more. For example, we often had people working on offshore projects for many weeks, away from their families. When one of them did a great job and the client was very satisfied, the department manager would meet with him or her and say, "Here's a $500 bonus. You did a fantastic job for us, and that helps build our reputation in the industry." That was a mini-review right there—with bonus. People didn't need to be anxious while waiting for an annual review, and the department managers didn't need to wrack their brains trying to recall every project that every person on their team had worked on in the previous twelve months. Everybody won.

• • •

At West Point, we learned about a psychology experiment where a chicken walks around a circle, and every time it reaches a certain point, a kernel of corn pops up. At first, the chicken moves quickly around the circle to get its reward. After a while, however, it figures out the game, and the chicken slows down to get to the kernel of corn only when it is hungry.

When the same experiment was run with the kernel of corn popping up at random intervals, the chicken moved quickly *all the time*. Obviously, I'm not comparing employees to chickens, but the psychology is interestingly similar: when people didn't know when they were going to receive bonuses or reviews, they tended to perform at a higher level consistently. At Mustang, they also knew that their leader had been thinking about them personally throughout the year. Isn't that what you want in your organization, too?

VALUE YOUR PEOPLE: GOOD EMPLOYEES ARE WORTH THEIR WEIGHT IN GOLD

Everything I've described so far in this chapter reflects our core philosophy about people: we *valued* them and told them so in many ways. Again, from the very beginning of our company, we were determined to be different by creating and maintaining trust and loyalty with our people. Therefore, right after our company was named, we came up with our company's credo: ***People Oriented ... Project Driven*™**. This was printed on all our company literature, right down to our business cards. This phrase immediately told people what Mustang stood for and summed up what we were all about: people and projects. That was our brand. It allowed us to start conversations about our core strength: a team culture with low turnover that produced great projects.

When we started Mustang, it seemed like many companies didn't value their employees, particularly their hourly people. Back

63

then, in Houston, this was especially true of engineers and designers, who felt like they were migrant workers in the oil and gas industry. Because I'm an engineer, I'll take myself out of this discussion, so let's just look at designers, who had no loyalty to any of the companies they worked for, because those companies had no loyalty to them. Many designers kept all their personal belongings in boxes under their desks, ready to go whenever they were let go or found a higher-paying job.

There was a design communication "grapevine," and designers all talked to one another about where they could earn more money. In boom times, designers would jump ship to earn a little more—even fifty cents more per hour, because that adds up if you're working fifty hours a week and getting paid time and a half for overtime. But then, during the industry's bust cycles, designers were usually the first people to be laid off.

As an engineering firm, it was important to have a strong reputation; and to meet that goal, we needed accurate drawings, which meant the *best* designers were needed. I learned this from my military background. The non-commissioned officers (NCOs) are the backbone of the army, because the officers are constantly being moved in and out as they are promoted and reassigned to advance their careers. The NCOs are the ones essentially running the organization on the ground, and they're the people who are teaching young officers how to do their jobs.

The designers were the NCOs in our industry. They were typically industry veterans who had worked on all types of projects for all the big companies, and they'd seen it all. Although many engineers treated designers like second-class citizens, we had enormous respect for them. So, when starting our company, one of our primary focus areas was raising design to a level of professionalism that hadn't been seen in the industry. We believed designers were as valuable as engineers, because again, if their drawings were correct, then our reputation in the fabrication yard and during startup for the client would be absolutely phenomenal. At Mustang, our focus was on the design room and changing how designers were treated from the beginning.

We didn't stop there, though, as *all* our people were valued. We didn't subscribe to the idea that people in some jobs were superior to others. We also challenged each person to learn more and move up to take on more responsibility.

WE DIDN'T SUBSCRIBE TO THE IDEA THAT PEOPLE IN SOME JOBS WERE SUPERIOR TO OTHERS. WE BELIEVED EVERYONE HAD THEIR OWN STRENGTHS, TALENTS, AND ABILITIES, WHICH WERE RESPECTED AND APPRECIATED.

Don't overlook your lower-paid hourly employees, as they are your backbone. Apply the same compensation principles that you do for your higher-salaried people to prevent them from leaving. Because we believed everyone had their own strengths, talents, and abilities, there was zero tolerance for putting people down.

KEEP THE BEST AND WINNOW THE REST

Much of what I've described so far in this chapter might sound very "warm and fuzzy," and many businesspeople may think you can't run a successful company (or any other organization) that way and still be successful when you get down to the bottom line of being profitable. Obviously, you need to be profitable, so you can stay in business and still have jobs for all those people. While firmly believing in taking care of the people, we always wanted to have *the best* people to work with.

To accomplish that goal, you need to do what we called "high-grading" of people. This term originated in forestry: it involves harvesting the highest grade of timber and leaving the less-well-developed trees behind. In our company, if there were good people who just weren't doing well on a particular project, managers moved them to another project, and if they succeeded there, they were fine. But if they didn't, they were moved out of the organization altogether. That may sound cold, but our team was managing a business, and companies need to be tough as nails to survive.

You may find the same situation in your organization. I admit it isn't easy letting people go; in fact, it is one of the hardest things any manager has to do. During startup, we thought the original people would be with us forever, but as the company grew, their responsibilities changed, and some people weren't changing fast enough to stay with us. One noticeable thing in the early days was that we were so short-staffed that everyone wore a lot of hats, so to speak, and they *loved* the constantly changing nature of their jobs. Then, as we grew, some of those jobs became more focused—and some of the people weren't happy about that change.

Also, as our company grew and changed, some people's skills or leadership ability didn't or couldn't grow to keep up with the new demands. We found that someone who managed two people in the beginning simply wasn't able to manage thirty people a few years later. Fortunately, many of our people could. One example was David Sneed, one of our first designers who grew along with the company to where he was ultimately running a department of a thousand people. But many people couldn't seem to make that kind of adjustment.

In other situations, people needed to keep up with changing technologies, and they were offered training to facilitate that. If they accepted our offer, they stayed on, but if they weren't willing to learn new things, our team needed to bring in people who were. That said, outgoing employees were always offered the opportunity to come back if they later acquired the knowledge, training, and experience needed. We were happy to see numerous motivated people do exactly that.

As mentioned, though, some people simply weren't a good fit with our culture. Some treated vendors badly, talking down to them and trying to take advantage of them. Others treated our clients poorly, ignoring their requests, which was counter to our inclusive, collaborative approach. Some had outstanding resumes and seemed exceptional in the interview, until we hired them and saw that they really didn't want to collaborate or cooperate with anyone else; they just wanted to be left alone. By now, you realize that's not how we worked or wanted to work.

Once identified, these people were removed quickly—even top project managers and sector managers who were responsible for bringing in clients and getting the work done. This spoke volumes to Mustangers when they saw managers they felt were "untouchable" being let go because of how they treated others. Fortunately, most of these "poor fits" left of their own volition, because they recognized that we weren't going to change Mustang's people-first culture. In a few cases, however, we had to initiate the separation.

We high-graded our people at all levels, in good times and bad. This habit helped us *stay lean in the good times* by keeping only the top talent and was a total game-changer in maintaining our readiness for the next inevitable downturn.

Our people weren't nervous when we fired employees who didn't fit our culture or talent requirements. Instead, it was viewed very positively because Mustangers wanted the company to stay strong and stay in business. Our people appreciated everything we did with our internal branding to maintain our healthy culture and ability to compete. They wanted us to be a "cycle-proof" company as that was good for everyone.

OBJECTIVE:

Break the code on building tight knit teams that take care of each other to become a Culture Code Champion. The increased energy in your teams will pull your people tighter together and increase your bottom line.

KEY POINTS TO KEEP IN MIND ON CRAFTING YOUR CULTURE:

1. "Culture eats strategy for breakfast." *Management guru Peter Drucker said this years ago, but it's still true today. A strong culture that everyone in your organization feels and believes in will do more for your organization's success than even the best strategy.*

2. Most people appreciate feeling as though they're part of a team. *Yet many companies or departments lack this sense of "team spirit." Find what makes your company or department different, and energize your people around that concept. It will pay off in ways you never imagined.*

3. Your company name is more important than you think. *Choose something people will identify with, that they'll call themselves, and that they'll rally around. We weren't "employees"; we were "Mustangers." People want to belong and to share that feeling of belonging with their coworkers.*

4. If you can't change the name of your organization, *choose a new name for your part of that organization. Create your own team with all the trappings (mottos, sayings, songs, traditions), and call it whatever works for you.*

5. Don't ignore the benefits of swag. *Put your logo on as many things as possible, and spread them throughout your company: T-shirts, hats, key chains, eyeglass cases, coffee mugs, drink holders—anything! This is such an inexpensive, tangible way of saying thank you to employees. Give them out as often as possible, to keep people talking and feeling that they belong and are appreciated.*

6. Have fun with your coworkers outside of work. *No one really wants to work for a company where they come in, work for eight hours (or more), and then just go home. Schedule events where people can get to know each other's families, outside interests, and hobbies. Organize activities where they can get to know each other as people, not just coworkers. By building relationships, you build great teams, inside and outside of work.*

7. Fun activities and charity events put smiles on people's faces and create lasting memories *for them and their families. They also provide content for young people to put on social media—which, by the way, makes their friends aware of the great company they are part of!*

8. Introduce your new employees to your culture right away, from day one. *New people especially need to feel that they belong, so they can start building relationships with others that will help them in their work and career. Start having a new-hire breakfast to thank people for joining and provide an opportunity for them to informally meet top management.*

9. Use hard-copy communication with your people and clients. *Everyone wants information, so give it to them, but by snail mail to your people's homes and to clients' offices, not by email. They and their spouses will read more of it and feel engaged. Win the hearts and minds of everyone you touch.*

10. Review performance regularly and often, not just once a year. *Reward people for a job well done when it's done, instead of months later. Give bonuses regularly, too. A little money throughout the year goes farther than a lump sum once a year.*

11. Rectify your hiring mistakes as soon as you recognize them. *Everyone will be better off. People who aren't a good fit for your company can find a place where they do fit well, and the people you already have will appreciate that you want to keep only the best. High-grade your people at all levels in good times and bad. This habit will help you stay lean in the good times, and it's a total game-changer.*

12. Value your people, and make sure they know you do with continuous touches. *Connecting with people is like piling sand and needs everyone's daily focus to help perpetuate the people-first culture. Win their hearts and minds to get passion ... passion moves the needle in building a team culture.*

CULTURE CODE CHAMPIONS WORKSHEET:
STEP 2: CREATE A SENSE OF TEAM

STRENGTH:
Internal:_____

_____

WEAKNESS:
Internal:_____

_____

OPPORTUNITY:
External:_____

_____

THREAT:
External:_____

_____

CHAMPION:
Hand Step 2 baton to: _____

Buddy: _____

Conceptual initial actions:

1. _____

2. _____

3. _____

4. _____

Start Date: _____

CHAPTER 3

CONTINUOUS SALES: SELL WHILE THE SHOP IS FULL

Continuous selling is not only the lifeline of your business, it is critical to developing a differentiated culture because it provides job security. Job security allows a culture to blossom.

No matter what business you're in or what function you have in that organization, sales is part of your job. Even if you're not selling your company's products or services to outside customers or clients, most people still need to have some sales savvy and skills to do their job. You need to sell your boss on giving you the go-ahead for your latest project or idea. You need to sell your coworkers on helping you accomplish your goals, since they don't answer to you—but their cooperation will help you succeed. You also "sell" your company in every interaction you have with the outside world. Sometimes the interaction is simply making a positive impression on people who will contribute to your organization's general reputation.

DO-IT-YOURSELF SALES

Although educated and trained as an engineer and leader, I had some experience in sales, but not much. I had worked in sales for six months early in my career during a tough time in the offshore oil and gas industry. Surprisingly, I found I enjoyed helping clients solve their technical problems as much as doing the actual engineering work.

When we started Mustang, I handled all the sales work due to my comfort with the job. In fact, we did not hire our first professional salesperson until we had been in business for seven years.

Many new businesses have the same challenge we had. They need to sell, but they don't have or can't afford any dedicated salespeople. Maybe you're a one-person company. Maybe you're a very small business, with only a few full-time people working with you. But even if you have hundreds or thousands of people in your organization, sales is still your most important function, because if you're not selling, there will be no need for your products or services. All those other people in your organization who are working in manufacturing, production, fulfillment, distribution, operations, marketing, advertising, finance, human resources, and other support roles will be sitting around idly while you go out of business.

Soon after starting Mustang, our designers told us that some of our competitors were struggling to find work. One company had four salespeople on staff and three fewer designers than us. Our staff consisted of twelve designers—and zero dedicated salespeople. Realizing that we were doing better than our competition without a sales team, we decided to stay that way. Having a full-time sales team just didn't fit in with our views on controlling—and minimizing—

overhead labor, lease space, and general expenses. We called these items "holes in the bucket" that could kill our profitability.

NARROW THE FIELD OF POTENTIAL SALES: FOCUS YOUR EFFORTS

What can you do if you don't have a dedicated sales force? You need to be smart about finding customers and convincing them to hire you. As mentioned in chapter 1, we decided to make a clean break from our previous employer and not take any people or projects with us. That was very different from what many startups do. Although this decision added a lot of stress, it forced us to be resourceful about finding our own projects and our own clients.

Our previous employer did help us, however unwittingly. The owners of that firm called all their clients to address the loss of three key engineers (us). They wanted to preempt the inevitable chatter in the industry as word spread that we had started our own firm. Their goal was to reassure their clients that we had left our projects in good shape and were not planning to poach people from them. Those calls were good for our former company's client relations, and they were also an absolute windfall for us. Why? Because when *we* started calling on potential clients, they already knew about us and were curious to find out more. They needed viable firms to compete for their work, and they knew of many firms that had closed or were closing. They wanted to know more about what Mustang was bringing to the table. The enthusiasm, energy, and earnestness with which we pitched ourselves came through over the phone, and we had a 100 percent hit rate on setting up visits with those clients. That was the first brick we laid in each new relationship with potential clients!

As a startup, we wouldn't be able to win large projects, as those were beyond our reach in the early days due to our small size. We were also missing some of the technical expertise required. Being realistic about our ability to win larger projects saved us a lot of sales time, proposal time, and aggravation. We needed customers and projects that "fit" us. No sense spending a lot of time that wouldn't pay off, even though those bigger clients with large projects wanted us to stretch ourselves and bid.

Instead, we focused on finding small projects at a select group of companies. Our targets were two major oil companies, four large independent oil companies, and eight small independent companies, because all of them had modification projects. This type of work was generally difficult to control and make a profit on. The projects would be tough, but they would be paying jobs that were under the radar of most of our competitors, and they would be bid and awarded in a matter of days. Often, those projects were of no interest to our competitors. In fact, in many cases, there was no competition for those projects at all. These projects were won on the basis of our reputation as individuals, until our new company had established a reputation of its own.

Focusing on small projects had other benefits as well. Obviously, if we finished the projects successfully, those clients would be more likely to call on us again. That facilitated *relationships built on performance*, which is an important way to build a business. Also, over time, those small projects became larger, and our clients felt comfortable awarding them to us because we had built trust.

We also wanted to avoid the mistakes other startup companies had made. The principals of other startups had hired themselves out as contract employees, working in other companies' offices. Although this was a good way to make money in the short term, it wasn't viable to sustain and grow their business in the long term. Clients saw those people as still working for someone else, instead of themselves, with no core team the client could count on. We wanted to *build* a sustainable business that would grow beyond us and succeed for many years in the future.

Our strategy for sales in the first few years was to sell our personal capabilities and leverage our relationships in the industry. One benefit of this approach was that it would control growth, since there would be no time for us to sell if we were busy working on projects. Handling the sales *and* the work ourselves ensured quality, saved us money on salespeople we couldn't afford, and conveyed a personal touch to our customers.

Keep this method in mind the next time your salespeople are out selling your products or services and making promises that don't match your capability. That happens all too often. When selling your *own* services, there is less chance to overpromise because *you* will be the one who has to deliver!

LEVERAGE YOUR NETWORK TO GET YOUR FOOT IN THE DOOR

When you can't throw money at a problem, you need to think smarter to figure out how to get things done. One way is to leverage your vendors to help find sales leads. We identified seventeen vendors who were beating the bushes hard, trying to sell valves, control panels, parts, and other equipment to the same companies we were hoping would hire us for project work. We had good relationships with our vendors' salespeople, and they had good relationships with clients, who often asked their opinion on which engineering firms could do a good job for them on upcoming projects.

We asked our vendors to simply find a way to mention Mustang when they were calling on their clients. We called this "same-sentence sales." We wanted them to mention Mustang in the same sentence as other, more-established companies that we would be competing with. This gave us some *credibility by association* with the vendor and the other companies mentioned. It improved our possibilities of getting the work, because our company name had been implanted in the client's mind as a viable option.

These vendors were confident that Mustang would take good care of clients, so they had no problem working our company's name into conversations with their customers. They often called us when they learned about new projects, and we shared information with them about what bids or other work we had heard about. This sharing of information kept us wired into what was happening in the industry. It also enabled us to make "rifle-shot" sales calls with clear, very precise targets to aim at. The vendor gave us information about the specific upcoming project at a particular company and who would be in charge. Additionally, they told us what the client's concerns were and what the vendor's strategy was to win the work.

For example, our company had been in business for six months when we got a call from one of our vendors, who had just finished a sales call with Conquest Exploration, a small independent oil company. The vendor told us Conquest wanted to add some equipment to two thirty-year-old Shell platforms that they had purchased, but they weren't sure if the structures could support the additional weight. The vendor told us he had mentioned our company's name in the "same sentence" with other possible firms that Conquest should consider working with. This happened in December, a notoriously difficult time to find work in our industry. Mustang needed the work, and I was excited that this vendor had mentioned us.

The story doesn't end there, of course. I called Conquest immediately, even though it was late afternoon on a Thursday, and I had never met the client. I call this approach "striking while the iron of courage is hot," and it has paid off for me many times. It paid off that day, too. I got through to the project leader, had a good conversation, and set up a meeting for the next day to discuss what he needed done. Apparently, he also believed in striking while the iron is hot!

Many people would have gone home that day, excited with the prospect of meeting a new potential client to sell them on hiring their company. But we went the extra mile. One of our core business philosophies was to do *"more than expected, better than expected."* Plus, we were hungry for work. So instead of simply preparing for a discussion about the platforms, we decided to create a fait accompli for getting the project. Our team stayed late into the wee hours of the morning, developing a computer presentation of exactly how we would analyze the platforms. The team essentially did 10 percent of the project before the first meeting. We did it because it seemed like the best way to win Conquest's trust for the project.

And it was!

Our contact at Conquest knew we were serious about the project even before we showed him our presentation, because the time of the meeting required us to navigate the horrendous rush-hour traffic in downtown Houston, on a Friday afternoon, no less.

But what really sold Conquest on us doing the project was the fact that we had taken the time to create a computer demonstration specific to Conquest's project. As they asked questions we were able to address them by manipulating the design analysis in real time. Our "just-do-it" work from the night before impressed Conquest, and they hired us on the spot. Even better, that led to more work later on for us, and the original vendor (who had mentioned our company name in "same-sentence sales") won the purchase order for all the equipment.

The point is that too many people call on potential clients without having done enough preparation to win the order. It's not enough to simply describe what you've done *before,* for *other* clients. The people you're meeting with want to know what you can and will do for *them.* That means you should do some of the work for that client, to show them that you're seriously interested in working with them. Demonstrate that you're willing to work hard to prove it to them—at your first meeting! We wanted to win work *without a bid process* whenever possible, and this is how we did it.

If you work in a business or for an organization where you don't have to prove yourself every time, and you can find new business just by sitting back and waiting for it, good for you. But for the rest of us, who want to win as much new business as possible, showing what you can do for each potential client is a smart way to close sales.

PARTNER WITH YOUR CUSTOMERS

Developing *trust* between companies and customers is a critical factor for any business relationship, even if you think your business consists solely of one-time transactions. Your first goal is always selling trust.

Whether you are selling automobile parts, clothing, computers, a financial product, or anything else, you want to earn your customer's trust, so they'll come back and buy from you again. If you're selling consulting services like we were, you want your clients' trust so that they'll hire you for the next project.

Earning clients' trust defined our business well. We wanted companies in the offshore oil and gas industry to hire us again and again and again: we called this "locking them up" (away from our competition). Repeat work from clients was more profitable for everyone involved due to a better starting point for communication.

• • •

Unfortunately, trust between clients and service companies had almost disappeared because of bad behavior (on both sides) during the 1970s boom and the 1980s bust cycles. To better understand this, let me provide a bit of background on how our industry traditionally did business in those days.

Most of the financial arrangements between clients and engineering companies were done on the basis of lump-sum, also known as fixed-price, contracting. Clients liked the lump-sum approach, because it put the risks on the contractors to assume the costs of any unforeseen or unknown costs that might occur during a project. They wanted contractors to have "skin in the game," so that both sides would be aligned on cost overruns hurting their respective businesses.

On the other side of the table, engineering companies also liked the lump-sum approach to contracting, because it allowed them to exclude their clients from the decision-making process, control the risks, and figure out for themselves how they could make a good profit on each contract.

Lump-sum contracts led to gamesmanship on both sides, which naturally destroyed trust between clients, engineers, vendors, and contractors. The "game" was generally around defining the scope of work with loopholes for price increases. Each company had to diligently and independently configure their scope of work, cost, pricing, and execution strategy to remain profitable in the industry. The mentality was definitely that the game was "win-lose," and each side obviously wanted to be the winner.

That's not the way we wanted to do business. Instead, we wanted Mustang to be built on reimbursable engineering, purchasing, and construction-management (EPCM) contracts and on trusting relationships that would be developed through performance of those contracts. Essentially, clients would be reimbursing us for time and materials, instead of paying a lump sum, which we felt was too risky for both us and our clients due to lack of definition at that early stage in the project. Then, later, we would bid the equipment and fabrication on behalf of the client. Those bids were lump-sum because we provided very detailed scopes of work. This strategy enabled us to help vendors reduce the contingency they put in their bids, which ultimately saved our client money.

The reimbursable approach fosters a true partnership with your customers, because you're working together in a collaborative manner to reduce the total project cost and schedule. Your customer saves money because you spend less time on that particular project, and your company is stronger because you can move on to the next project. We wanted to do more projects and gain efficiencies rather than expand the projects we had—which was very different from our competitors who focused on expanding projects.

When we started using this approach, there was only about $20 million worth of reimbursable work in our *industry* worldwide. Yet twenty years later, when our company reached $1 billion in revenue, the entire billion dollars was reimbursable. We had helped move the industry to "win-win" contracting.

• • •

So, what does all this have to do with sales? *Everything.*

When you are selling lump-sum services work, the bid award is often based more on price than on capability because the scope of work is not fully defined. These awards can very easily end up in court if the contractor gets into trouble with its cost during the execution of the project.

In contrast, reimbursable services are based on a detailed scope of work. This type of contract award will be based more on the team's capability and trust. The contract is actually a mini-alliance to get the work done as a collaborative team. We were able to put our contracts in the drawer and never go to court!

BUILD TRUST WITH CLIENTS BY *NOT* ALWAYS SELLING

One of the ways we built trust is that we didn't try to grab everything for our company. Instead, when working with a client and talking about a project and how to execute it, we offered other options the client might consider for engineering, as well as for construction, and showed them what the cost differences would be.

Once, during a meeting with our client's managers, we recommended that they hire another engineering firm for part of their project. We told them, "You should buy this structural design from this other engineering firm, because it is a good design, and it's available. Then we'll just do the equipment-deck design and manage the project for you." This client-focused honesty earned Mustang their trust, and ultimately they ended up forcing us to do the extra scope anyway!

Another time, we met with one of the district managers for ARCO, who said he wanted all his projects done by our company, because he felt that he would receive tremendous value for the money spent. Although this was gratifying to hear, we told him that while Mustang would be happy to take on *many* of his projects, we couldn't do all of them, for several reasons. First, there would be times when we wouldn't be able to staff a job due to our workload, so he needed to maintain relationships with other firms. Secondly, the big companies like his want to bid to several companies regularly, to ensure that they're getting the best value. Even though we would provide excellent value, he wouldn't want to be second-guessed by his own upper management, who might question why he was sending all his work to one company.

Sales used this "pass the work around" speech thousands of times, to help build credibility and trust with our clients. We truly wanted them to be successful long term, so we coached them whenever it might be helpful. Clients didn't hear this type of advice from our competitors, who always tried to limit the playing field, not expand it. Our people-first mentality included making our clients heroes.

My point is that by *not* trying to secure *all* the work for a particular client, but instead recommending who or what would be the *best solution* for that client, we fostered a lot of trust. They understood that we were open and inclusive with other companies in our industry, and that we were willing to bring in and work with other companies that would benefit them. In short, we were willing to share. Many businesses become so driven to win that they lose out on the opportunity to be a *key cog* in an industry team. Often, they think they are the only ones who can do something right, and they certainly want all the revenue. Many were set up as a one-stop shop offering engineering, procurement, construction, and installation. We liked doing what we were best at and sharing the rest with other companies. This allowed us to work on *more* projects and cultivate more relationships that would produce future work.

Paul, Felix, and I believed in the win-win approach to business (and life), and that's the way we ran our business. By giving clients the names of people they should use at other companies we not only showed a deep knowledge of our industry, we also demonstrated a true focus on our clients' needs. This showed that we were realistic about our own capabilities and we declined to take on so much work that our quality would suffer.

This overriding philosophy of sharing built trust, which is critical to sales, good business, and the ability to sleep at night.

It's very difficult to do, but sometimes it's best to turn away work altogether—if it's not the right project for you. Several years ago, we got a call from a retired US Air Force officer, who said he could help us win a bid for a plant upgrade in California. However, we were based in Houston, and all the people currently working on that project were onsite in California. He contacted us because he said he had heard that Houston firms had the lowest overhead markups anywhere in the country. He believed the low overhead would create the value proposition he needed to win the contract for us.

While we were flattered to be invited to join his project, we knew it wasn't right for us. We hadn't done any work for the government, but we knew it would be paperwork-intensive, and there were other opportunities that were a better fit for us. We declined to bid, but we gave him the names of other firms in Houston that did onshore plant work and wished him the best.

As it turned out, one of my neighbors (whom we recommended) prepared a bid for him and put thirty people to work in California on a three-year project, at an above-average profit. Obviously, that would have been a nice addition to our company's bottom line, but our job was resource allocation to create a profit. We had to evaluate opportunities, make decisions, and move on to the next hot prospect. There was just too much going on for us to worry about lost opportunities like this one.

You can't chase them all, and you shouldn't. As mentioned earlier in this chapter, you need to narrow your sales efforts and focus on the work or opportunities that you know your organization can do best. Don't take on work you won't do well, because in the long run that will only hurt you and your organization's reputation.

BUILD A BRAND TO INCREASE REPEAT BUSINESS

I mentioned the use of swag in chapter 2. For clients, we chose things they would actually use. Since those items were branded with our company name and logo, we hoped clients would think of us every time they used them. I listed many of those items earlier, because they're crucial to building an internal brand and a team culture, but here are a few more examples of some of the things that worked well for us with clients.

We gave away calculators. (Of course: we're engineers!) We also gave away calendars—yes, calendars. We know clients used them, because we saw our calendars in hundreds of offices and conference rooms. After all, people need *visual* calendars, especially when they're planning projects that will roll out over many months or even years. If you make your calendars attractive enough, your customers will be happy to put them up. Our calendars featured our logo—the blue mustang—but in a very subtle way, screened in the background. Our company name was at the top, and our calendar didn't look like an advertising piece. Also, our calendars were *huge*—two feet by three feet—and they were laminated and came with a marker so that clients could use them immediately for planning.

Don't be so quick to decide that this type of thing is silly, or not appropriate for your business, or would not be welcomed by your customers or clients. After all, these were developed for a services firm, and we worked on multi-billion-dollar projects. Figure out what will work for you. We were serious about the quality of our work, but we were also serious about reminding clients to call us first when they needed what we did best. Mustang wanted to be first choice! All those calendars, calculators, letter openers, coffee mugs, toys, and hats helped do exactly that: thank our clients for working with us and reminding them that they should call *us*.

That approach can work for you, too, so think about how you can brand your company or organization and what swag you can come up with that will remind *your* customers of what you do best. What will stay on their desks or in their offices or be taken home?

WIN CUSTOMERS BY DIFFERENTIATING YOURSELF

Handling all the sales by myself for the first seven years was a great way for our company to differentiate itself. I was one of the owners, and the initial contact. Our customers *loved* that, because they weren't talking to a sales-y type salesperson; they were meeting with someone who was fully invested in the success or failure of the business.

Whenever possible, try to make personal sales calls on potential customers. That personal connection inspires trust in you, and it creates a stronger bond and a stronger relationship with your customers. It's an excellent way to grow your client base and get referred business. As I've said many times, "Good things happen when you make sales calls," because you are out learning something new that could lead to work.

Eventually, your organization will grow to the point where you'll need a dedicated sales force to develop relationships with your customers. If you hire right, you'll have outstanding people in place who can continue what you've been doing for your company.

However, that doesn't mean you have to step away from sales altogether. Even after our company had a large staff of talented, professional salespeople, my partner and I still met with clients regularly. We wanted to get direct feedback on how our teams were performing. At other times, we helped close the deal, especially on huge projects with international companies. Paul and I could bring a lot of our history to bear in these conversations, since we had been involved from the beginning of the company, and our commitment to strong teams came through.

In addition to having the owners involved in technical work, management, and sales, we also were able to differentiate our company in other ways. Here are a few: 1) Our teams had long tenure and strong performance. 2) More than 100 different clients had used us multiple times. 3) We proved we were innovative, with our brains turned on, by using examples from previous work. 4) There were more than eighty projects with first-time technology that set performance benchmarks in the industry. 5) Also, we made our computer systems user-friendly and nonproprietary, so our clients could continue to use them without us, which they appreciated! Think about and list the various ways you differentiate your company from your competition.

Client-oriented performance by strong teams was a differentiator for our sales team.

HIRING SALESPEOPLE TO INCREASE GROWTH

Of course, with growth comes the need for more people. One thing our customers eventually noticed was that the only time they saw me was to close a sale. I was busy doing so many things that I typically called on clients only when there was potential work—a rifle shot sales call as discussed earlier. After we got the work, I turned it over to operations. I'm not the type of person who calls on clients merely to visit; I called them if I had a reason to see them.

But as our business and company grew, clients wanted to see more of me. They wanted to visit regularly; they wanted to know what was going on with Mustang, so they could continually assess our capabilities. They wanted more of an information flow, because they knew I talked to their competitors, and they wanted my take on what was

WHEN YOU BUILD TRUST AND A RELATIONSHIP WITH A CLIENT, YOU NEED TO MAINTAIN THAT RELATIONSHIP.

happening in the industry. When you build trust and a relationship with a client, you need to maintain that relationship. So, by the time our company had grown to 250 people with fifty-plus clients, we knew it was time to hire a salesperson to help cover that client base.

As discussed in chapter 1, we strongly believed in hiring referrals from people we already worked with and respected. When word got out that we were looking for a professional salesperson, one of our trusted project managers, Dick Westbrook, suggested an interview with one of his friends, Jim Vogt. Jim had been laid off from an engineering and construction company, where he had been in charge of sales. We were more than willing to talk to him, because we strongly believed in hiring good people who had been let go from other firms in our very cyclical and unpredictable industry.

Jim had been told that we needed someone to touch base regularly with fifty to seventy clients. In fact, we didn't even need him to sell anything for the next six to eight months, because Mustang had plenty of projects and clients backlogged. That was helpful, because it allowed him to come in and get to know our company, as well as time to develop relationships with our clients without pressure. He requested that I go with him on initial sales calls to work the handoff of my relationship and set him up for success. He knew some clients might resist the handoff from an owner, and he wanted to nip that in the bud.

Hiring Jim as our first salesperson had another unforeseen benefit. He introduced us to Mary Needham, who still heads an executive-search firm. She is based in Houston and specializes in the oil and gas industry. Although Jim had been recommended by one of our employees, he had a contract with Mary, so I met with her to discuss Jim's capabilities.

Mary confirmed that Jim was the right salesperson to help us identify more projects to choose from, and we hired him. A year later, we were looking for a salesperson to help us penetrate the major oil companies, and she recommended Dennis Frakes. He developed relationships that Jim and I would not have had the time or ability to do, and he helped our company make headway with projects for the major oil companies.

From 2002 to 2007, we expanded to twenty-three salespeople, and I gradually turned things over to them, using a "Full-Throttle" initiative, which I'll explain later in this chapter.

INCREASE SALES BY DIVERSIFYING INTO NEW MARKETS

When you first start a business, you're likely to take whatever work comes along. Everyone I've ever talked to who has started a business admits to this—and it doesn't matter *what* industry. In general, that's not a bad way to get started, but many people find that, over time, they either settle into the core business they wanted, or they get pulled into a direction they had never anticipated.

That's how we started, too—intentionally. We never felt that we could push a direction. Instead, we simply went wherever the industry projects pulled us. In other words, we were reactive rather than proactive—and that served us very well for a while. We had followed vendors, contractors, and even clients into international work, and some of it was for major oil companies.

But we wanted to do *more*.

• • •

For the first eight years or so, our company worked on *upstream projects*. In our industry, upstream work involves production of oil and natural gas from wellheads onshore and offshore. The oil and natural gas are transported by pipeline or tanker to downstream gas plants or refineries. There the oil or natural gas is split into constituent parts for use or for further processing. Refineries produce gasoline or diesel and by-products that go into chemical plants. Finally, the chemical plants make all manner of materials to use in producing everything from plastic to nylon products.

We didn't pursue diversifying into downstream until we hired our first two professional salespeople, Jim and Dennis. Both of them had extensive experience in downstream work, and that helped us get started in broadening the company's scope of expertise. A few years later, we brought in the Litwin crew (as described in chapter 1), and we were a full-fledged downstream project firm.

Diversification is often difficult because it typically requires your top people, and it may not be initially profitable. We found that when we assigned a *team to champion* a new venture, it always succeeded, because that team knew how to get the support required. Assigning a team to champion any new initiative was one of our key lessons learned. Once you prove you can produce in the new area reliably, many opportunities will find you because a business that does what it says it will do is rare and very much sought after.

When these opportunities arise, you need to evaluate how each opportunity will mesh with what you are doing and what the barrier to entry is. We often found that we could push back on an opportunity and refuse to accept it, unless the parameters were changed to lower the barrier to entry and our risk. If you have a situation like this and your client agrees to your requirements, you have a good indication that the client is eager to work with a new company and will likely help you be successful. This worked for us in the chemical industry where we found clients who just wanted a new company for a fresh start and hopefully better performance.

WIN THE TIES

Normally bids come down to two players, because the client needs to maintain options to the end. Our goal was always to "win the ties." That is where you actually close the sale.

You have to figure out what it takes to win the tie, and it isn't just price. By this point, you will have played all your cards to differentiate from your competition, and the client needs to make the final decision.

In the army, we learned that "energy and enthusiasm is a force multiplier" on the battlefield. At Mustang, we worked to demonstrate we had that energy and enthusiasm in team members who had worked together repeatedly and who communicated well. Emphasizing this enthusiastic team culture to our clients won many ties.

Our first experience of winning the tie was for Houston's Metro bus company soon after we started Mustang. We were the only offshore-engineering firm bidding, but we had solid checkmarks in every area the client evaluated. We would be the last firm to present, right before lunch, and believed we would probably get only a cursory look before Metro awarded to one of its usual firms.

But their project people wanted a firm like ours because of recent safety problems incurred from their usual design firms. The six-person board was not all technical people, however, and would need convincing. We went into a formal setting with them on one side of the room, and us on the other.

I flipped our first chart over and it said, "Mustang will satisfy you," similar to the Snickers candy bar jingle. Then I broke all the rules and walked over to their table and started putting a big Snickers bar in front of each person while saying they were going to hear about a different type of engineering firm that was totally geared toward taking care of them.

I worked my way down to the last person, who was a few months pregnant but not showing. (I had a friend at Metro who had let me know of her announcement.) After putting a big Snickers bar in front of her, I pulled a small one out of the bag and said it was for her baby.

This got everyone laughing, which changed the energy in the room. Laughter opens people to change, and then you can redirect them to think differently. We moved from a presentation to a discussion of how we could best help each other. And we won the tie!

Metro saved us because there was no offshore work to do. To this day, Mustang still has small Snickers bars at every function and at many presentations. They are there to remind everyone to be "other-oriented" and take care of each other. "Mustang will satisfy you" became part of the lore of Mustang.

TEAMING WITH THE BOY SCOUTS HELPED DEVELOP OUR SALES PROGRAM

During a severe oil-price downturn, the Sam Houston Area Council (SHAC) of the Boy Scouts asked me to invigorate its year-long Friends of Scouting (FOS) fundraising drive. This drive collected small amounts ($1–$50) from family and friends of scouting. There was a separate fundraising effort for corporations. The downturn was making it difficult for them to meet their goal of $640,000, which would reduce the camping and activities SHAC could provide for more than 130,000 scouts. Dena Lee brought her marketing team to help Mustang-ize the program and create a "Full-Throttle" racing theme to make the monthly report meetings fun for the district leadership teams.

The district leaders agreed to put on hats each month to show how they felt their program was progressing. There was a pit-crew hat to say they needed help, a smoking-the-tires hat for getting going, a full-throttle hat for making progress, and a checkered-flag hat for meeting the district goal. The district leaders also gave examples of something that had worked well for them in order to cross-train those ideas with the other districts. We not only eliminated district competition, but got them all helping each other. Once, two districts sent people over to help a district that was wearing the "need help" pit-crew hat. They helped that lagging district catch up over the next month!

We challenged ourselves to also change the FOS drive from twelve months to five, with a celebration dinner in mid-May. A shorter schedule would free up the unit leaders to focus on camping in the summer and recruitment/advancement in the fall, which would be a huge win for the entire scouting program. Gifts increased

60 percent in three years (to more than $1 million) and the "Full-Throttle" program went nationally to all councils. It was fun for us to implement Mustang's cross-training, team-building, and hero-making culture-building methods in the FOS Scouting organization. The result was better leadership teams in scouting—and, of course, a better scouting program for the boys.

TEAM SALES CREATE MORE HORSEPOWER

There are always problems in communication between sales and operations. Our managers found that teaching and implementing a recognized sales process (we used Miller Heiman) solved much of this by providing a common language and a structure for advancing the prospect to a closed sale. Marketing brought the Full-Throttle program created for the Boy Scouts back to Mustang as a sales strategy, with teams built around each of our salespeople, as diagrammed on the following page:

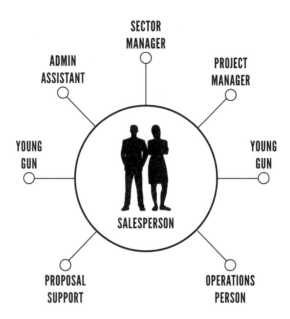

Each team had a talented driver (the salesperson) and a pit crew for support and for celebrating the win. Like everything in the company, the sales process was used to cross-train between groups, increase communication, and provide transparency. Information is power, and we wanted to prevent "power channels" in the company.

The sales team concept was also used to provide mentoring to our "Young Guns" and get them involved in sales early in their careers.

The sales process we selected gave names to the players on the client's side and one of them was called a "coach." The coach is someone who thinks your company is the right answer for his or her company and will provide background information that may help you win. We wanted to develop a number of these coaches at different levels in all client organizations by using our administrative assistants, young guns, designers, engineers, and managers to develop relationships.

• • •

For example, Exxon wanted to Mustang-ize its $500 million Diana project in 1997. Major projects always had names … this one started producing in 2003. Industry benchmarks had proven that our team culture reduced total project cost and schedule by 30 percent. The benchmarking company stated that having vendors and clients on our team was a critical factor in these savings. All of the major oil companies had come to us basically saying they needed to somehow Mustang-ize their project-delivery processes, or they were not going to survive long term. They were absolutely correct, as over the next few years, they combined to form ExxonMobil, BP/Amoco, Chevron Texaco, etc. At the time, we were too far down the food chain to believe this would happen—but we definitely wanted to help them improve their project metrics!

Diana would be the deepest drilling and production platform in the world, located 200 miles south of Houston in 4,800 feet of water. It would be our first-ever bid to Exxon, and we were anxious to show the Exxon managers what we could do to change their benchmarks for cost and schedule. However, they sent out an onerous bid package that would force bidders to do it their way. At that time, a project manager told me their idea of "win-win" was that Exxon wins twice!

We turned in a noncompliant bid for a Mustang-type project-execution strategy. A "coach" we had on the inside called a few days later to tell me our bid was in the trash can and why.

The good news was that they had read it first and felt we were too overloaded to do the project. We sent in some additional information to solve that concern, and we came back out of the trash can. This happened two more times before Exxon picked us to do the job.

Then Exxon's drilling team discovered the Hoover reservoir located very close to Diana and decided to combine the production into one massive production facility. The project became twenty times more difficult as the concept changed, becoming the world's largest and deepest floating complex. "Diana/Hoover" would ultimately produce 100,000 barrels of oil a day (5 percent of the entire production in the Gulf of Mexico) and had enough power-generation capacity to power the city of Austin, Texas. It was a floating city with living accommodations for over one hundred people and a full drilling rig. Many science projects moved from the lab to the real world on that project, requiring close coordination and communication between hundreds of companies.

CREATING A TEAM SALES PROGRAM AROUND A RECOGNIZED SALES PROCESS WILL *MINT YOU MONEY.*

Exxon normally runs 30–80 percent over budget on projects like these, as revealed in their internal benchmarking. We got engineering off of the project's critical path (people did not think we could do this with a major oil company) and helped bring it in under budget. The "coach" in Exxon had been right in helping us win the project, which saved them about $100 million according to benchmarks.

• • •

When our Full-Throttle teams won a project, they would take a sports car over and get the client's team outside for a picture—normally with everyone pushing the car together. We wanted to put a smile on everyone's face and create a memory as we started a new project together. We always said, "Celebrate what you want to see more of," and we loved winning projects for great clients. Finally, we gave framed pictures to everyone on the team!

Creating a team sales program around a recognized sales process will *mint you money.* Sales and operations will be aligned on what to chase and how to chase it. The relative strengths of the relationship-building salesperson and the very capable project managers will be brought to bear on the right actions to deliver continuous wins.

CROSS-TRAINING BY SHARING CONTACTS ACROSS COMPANIES

After selling to Wood Group, headquartered in Aberdeen, Scotland, in 2000, we invited Wood Group's salespeople to join our monthly golf association. Wood Group owned more than sixty companies, and eight of them were in Houston. While riding with one of the salesmen, I complained about not being able to get in to see a certain company CEO in New Orleans. I was shocked when he said, "Oh, I can get you in to see him whenever you want; he was my college roommate!" Wow, what an eye-opener: even though his company performed different services than our company, there was overlap in clients we could leverage together.

Internally, we had been cross-training our salespeople to share contacts between upstream, mid-stream, downstream, pipeline, and automation. This took some work; salespeople do not normally want to share their best contacts, because they are concerned another group will mess up and cause them embarrassment. After some training to get the salespeople comfortable that each area of our company was indeed the best in that part of the industry, they opened up, and the tight contacts delivered many easy wins: more than $15 million in revenue in the first twenty months.

At a meeting with the CEOs and top salespeople of the Houston-based Wood Group companies, it was surprising to learn the CEOs also didn't want to share their best contacts. This was the same hurdle we had faced internally between business units. After about six months of work and training, just as we had done internally at Mustang, everyone became comfortable and started sharing. It seemed like every salesperson had ten to fifteen supertight contacts that they could get in to see at any time. These contacts were used to introduce the other companies and services offered by Wood Group. We started celebrating the wins from this effort, and they soon bloomed from $20 million to more than $140 million per year in revenues to the participating companies.

This is a major extension of using your vendors for "same-sentence sales" and is another avenue for finding work. We called this effort "Joined Up Thinking." Can you partner with other companies to share sales relationships and grab some low-hanging fruit?

SELL WHILE THE SHOP IS FULL

One Friday, the phone rang off the hook and we were awarded seven projects. Over the weekend, we worked to figure out if we could do all this work without messing something up.

We had to take four of the projects for repeat clients to lock them in to our responsiveness. As I've said before, we loved to be first choice and "lock up clients" so that our competitors could not shake them.

Of the three new clients, we decided to turn down Pete Peterson's at Bellnorth Oil & Gas. Pete was very experienced in the industry, and we knew he could get his work done by another firm.

Dave Rucker and I went to see Pete on Tuesday to let him know we had been awarded too much work on Friday and that we needed to turn down his award. There was no building security back then, so we just walked in and went to Pete's office, which was full of people. We motioned for him to come out into the hall, and we pitched our sad story.

To our shock, he said that all the people in his office were actually there for the kickoff meeting! So, it was time for some quick thinking. We knew that the job had standard equipment that would not require much engineering to go out for bid by using our experienced purchasing people (cross-training to the rescue!). We asked him if we could define the equipment now in the kickoff meeting and then we would have purchasing go straight out for bids. By the time the bids would come in, we would have engineering available to help with the bid evaluation, conditioning and award.

Pete agreed, so we had a detailed kickoff meeting. It was a little embarrassing back in the office when we had to admit that we had failed in our mission. At first, the lesson learned seemed to be that it is never a good idea to send a sales guy to turn down work!

However, this project award actually showed us that there were lots of ways to do a project if the client really wanted you. Surprisingly, Pete's project was completed for 60 percent of our estimate, because our team was overloaded and only did what was absolutely required. We called this "fit-for-purpose" design, a no-frills approach.

Selling while the shop was full also provided great stories for salespeople. Our people would be upbeat about everything going on and they could show new efficiencies or concepts we had developed. This slight overload also kept us running lean and hard in the good times. This was a huge advantage in terms of being ready for the next downturn.

We provided new efficiencies (to reduce man hours) and new technical designs to salespeople from operations. We called these "arrows in the quiver" for them to go hunt with. The fun name kept operations people working to find more arrows for the salespeople to use and fostered more cooperation. With this information and a positive outlook, our salespeople brought more value to client meetings, helping them to open any door.

In order to support our culture, we had to always be selling. In our industry, projects would occasionally be cancelled overnight, because the oil price had plummeted or because of politics. There is a tendency for management to focus on work when the shop is full, but that just sets up an internal downturn in work when projects approach the finish line. The "job on the corner of the desk" (described in chapter 1) was a critical component of retaining our employees and developing our culture of strong teams that completed jobs more efficiently. Continuous selling while the shop was full helped us "cycle-proof" the company and stay lean in the good times. This strategy allowed us to not go down when the industry did; we firmly believed there was no reason that we had to go down if we had the right habits. Continuous selling is not only the lifeline of your business; it is critical to developing a differentiated culture because it provides job security.

CONTINUOUS SELLING IS NOT ONLY THE LIFELINE OF YOUR BUSINESS; IT IS CRITICAL TO DEVELOPING A DIFFERENTIATED CULTURE ...

OBJECTIVE:

Break the code on continuous productive selling to become a Culture Code Champion. The increased efficiency and the job security your people feel will increase your bottom line.

CONTINUOUS SALES: SELL WHILE THE SHOP IS FULL

KEY POINTS TO KEEP IN MIND ABOUT CONTINUOUS SALES:

1. If you run a business or lead any other type of organization, sales is part of your job. *You need to sell your organization's mission to potential clients, employees, and the general public, in order to spread the word about what you do and how you're better or different.*

2. Focus your sales efforts. *It is especially important to be smart when you don't have a huge sales force. Don't waste time chasing projects you're not likely to get. Be realistic, prove yourself on work you can get, and those successes will lead to more and/or bigger wins.*

3. Use your network to get your foot in the door with clients. *We called this "same-sentence sales." Ask your vendors to simply mention your name to potential clients during their sales meeting and then notify you. Then you are set up for a "rifle-shot sales call," after you've learned from the vendor what you need to know about the project, the client, and the client's key concerns.*

4. Partner with your customers to reduce their costs and yours. *This may sound counterintuitive, but it's a better approach that provides more work (and happier customers) in the long run. By using "reimbursable contracting" and creating true win-win situations, we helped change the way our industry did business. We made clients part of our team.*

5. Don't oversell your clients. *Build trust by not always promoting your services (especially if you're not right for the project). If you refer clients to other companies, they'll recognize that you have their best interests at heart. Your willingness to share will pay off over time.*

6. Make your company impossible to forget. *Give clients swag, to remind them of you when they're looking for help: pens, calculators, desk accessories, toys for their kids, whatever is useful or just plain fun that helps you stand out from everyone else.*

7. Know what makes you different from your competition—*which sounds basic—but reinforce that every time you interact with clients and potential clients. Once you create a winning culture similar to Mustang's, it will be a key differentiator.*

8. Recognize when you need to expand. *When you're just starting out, you will have to wear many hats and handle many different functions. But as your business grows, you should be aware of when you need help. Be willing to hire people who are better than you to help you maintain strong client relationships. Don't continue to go it alone, because those relationships will suffer.*

9. Evaluate each opportunity for diversification in your client base to ensure it matches your strengths. *Be willing to go where the industry needs you, but make sure that fits your overall goals. Turn down work that does not "fit." Assign a team to champion each new diversification venture to ensure success.*

10. Win the ties that invariably come about in all bids after an evaluation process. *Energy and enthusiasm from teams that have worked together can tip the scale in your favor.*

11. Create a team sales program around a recognized sales process. *Getting sales and operations aligned with a common sales language and plan will provide transparency and predictability. Invite nonsalespeople to the party.*

12. Sell while the shop is full to ensure you can take care of your people—*the industry does not really care if you survive. It is up to you to ensure continuity for your people and teams across industry cycles. The possible overload at times will increase efficiency and keep you lean in the good times—this is a total game changer.*

CULTURE CODE CHAMPIONS WORKSHEET:
STEP 5: SELL WHILE THE SHOP IS FULL

STRENGTH:
Internal:_____
_____

WEAKNESS:
Internal:_____
_____

OPPORTUNITY:
External:_____
_____

THREAT:
External:_____
_____

CHAMPION:
Hand Step 5 baton to: _____
    Buddy: _____
Conceptual initial actions:
    1. _____
    2. _____
    3. _____
    4. _____
Start Date: _____

CHAPTER 4

BUST SILOS: GET EVERYONE WORKING TOGETHER

Many organizations today are structured in ways that resemble silos, like a farm silo that stores grain. The term is used to visualize organizations that group people together by function. With this structure, marketing people work in the marketing department, finance people in the finance department, and so forth, and the departments are usually physically separated, as well. For example, marketing might be on one floor and operations on another. Sometimes, different departments are in different corners of the building. And sometimes, different departments are in different buildings—or even cities, states, or countries.

Managers often structure their companies this way because they're easier to manage: each silo runs its own business as efficiently as possible and then reports out at the top. That may seem like a practical way to organize, and it may be an easier structure to manage, but it's not the way people work together best. The boundaries inhibit or stop free communication.

To better understand this problem—so you can avoid or prevent it—this chapter first looks at all the difficulties that silos present, and then offers some solutions that were proven effective for us.

PROBLEMS CREATED BY SILOS

Silos create more problems than they solve or eliminate. Organizing people to work in different departments and physical areas actually prevents teamwork, in the following ways:

- Silos create rework.
- Silos foster elitism.
- Silos foster competition between your people, instead of collaboration.
- Silos lead to "unobtainium," which I'll define soon.
- Silos create finger-pointing and blame.

Let's take a closer look at each of these problems, because the better you understand them, the more you can either avoid or eliminate them.

SILOS CREATE REWORK

Before starting our company, we evaluated how other engineering firms were organized. In all cases, the results were counterproductive for communication. For example, in one company, the structural engineers worked in one hallway, but equipment engineers worked in another, and purchasing was on a different floor. This was inefficient, because these people had to work *together* on projects, but since they worked nowhere near each other, there was a lot of missed communication, and many things needed to be reworked and redone. That costs money and time, which affected everyone working on the project as well as the client, who had to deal with delays.

Our primary business was the design of offshore oil platforms, where every square foot of space is extremely expensive, weight has to be controlled, and equipment is packed in very tightly. To do that, the structural engineers worked to optimize their structural design, which would have a lot of diagonal struts between equipment deck levels to save steel. However, if there are a lot of diagonals, then the equipment won't fit in efficiently, or not at all! As a result, after the structural design was finished, the equipment engineers would require the structural engineers to rework parts of the design to open up space.

At the same time, both groups were typically sending requests to the purchasing department to buy what they needed—but then all the changes made the purchasing people seem incompetent, because they had to keep changing what was out for bid with their vendors. Studies of multiple projects provided a conservative estimate that most designs were redone *seven times* from concept through start-up—all because of poor communication among the many groups and companies involved. That's a lot of rework! And a lot of inefficiency. But if the structural engineers and equipment engineers had simply worked together on the design from the beginning, there wouldn't have been any need for extensive rework; in fact, only two partial redesign efforts would have been required due to purchasing or construction input.

SILOS FOSTER ELITISM

In many companies, the owners are located in a different place from the rest of the company. They have better offices, better carpet, and better furniture, which further separates them from everyone else. That type of separation doesn't create a sense of teamwork. In fact, it does exactly the opposite by creating a physical barrier to communication. It makes for hands-off ownership and puts all the responsibility for reporting and profitability on the department managers.

SILOS FOSTER COMPETITION BETWEEN YOUR PEOPLE, INSTEAD OF COLLABORATION

All this separation creates a sense of internal competition, instead of collaboration. In many organizations, I've seen HR pitted against the corporate communications department, or marketing vs. sales, or new-product development vs. manufacturing. A spirit of competition is innate in many people, but you don't want your people competing with *each other*—which is likely what they'll do if they're not working together, collaboratively. Instead, you want your people to compete with *your competitors!* You want your organization operating as one big team, and to do that, you need to get rid of that "us vs. them" mentality that can break down and fragment a company.

SILOS LEAD TO "UNOBTAINIUM"

People working in silos also don't understand or appreciate what people who work in other silos need in order to do their parts of the job correctly, the first time. For example, many times engineers created designs that required equipment that was not standard, which caused enormous problems for purchasing. Purchasing found it difficult—and sometimes impossible—to source that equipment.

Our purchasing people came up with a clever name for such equipment—and the problem that created it—by calling it "unobtainium," a new element on the periodic table:

Like the name suggests, *unobtainium* is something completely *unobtainable* in the real world. It can appear in any type of company or organization, and I'm sure you can think of a few examples in your organization. Perhaps someone has requested a report with data that requires a herculean effort to acquire and compile, for example.

Most of the time the person requesting *unobtainium* has no idea that it's unobtainable. When people work closely together throughout a project, however, unobtainium is revealed very early on, before it becomes a huge problem. This early communication across silos will prevent having to start over from scratch, costing you and your client money. Rework is an efficiency and profit killer.

SILOS CREATE FINGER-POINTING AND BLAME

Another problem with silos is they create what we call "the Dunce Syndrome"—which is closely related to *unobtainium*. A *dunce* is a person considered incapable of learning. When one department hands off part of a project to another department, projects can stall because the second department couldn't work with what the first department had created. We actually heard people saying things like *"Why aren't those dunces doing anything with the information we gave them?"* They felt that they had given the other group everything they needed, but they were just incapable of using it.

Of course, those people weren't "dunces;" they just couldn't work with the information they had been given from the first department, because it wasn't *in the form or level of completeness* that they needed. Instead, they had to figure out a way to transform that information into the form or format that they could work with. This naturally took time (and sometimes creativity and ingenuity). When you get rid of the silos, you get rid of the blame. People who work together, instead of separately in their own little world, have a better understanding of what their coworkers need, and then they can all work efficiently due to better handoffs.

BUSTING SILOS BY CO-LOCATING TEAMS

We were determined to bust the silos that had created communication problems and inefficiency in other companies. From the very beginning, all people who were working on a project were located in one physical area. That meant that whoever was doing the design, engineering, purchasing, and construction management were all together in the same space, so they could work *together* on the project.

This not only improves communication; it also fosters a greater sense of teamwork: after all, it's hard to have an "us vs. them" mentality when you're all in the same room!

Of course, this is easy when you don't have a lot of people working in your organization, and it does become a bit more challenging when there are dozens, or hundreds, or thousands of people working for a single company. But we continued to do it, even as our company grew—and growth was fast. Here's a short overview:

- Day one: it was only the three of us—Felix, Paul, and me—in 1,200 square feet on the first floor of a two-story building. There were two two-person offices, one single office, and an open area for ten wooden drafting tables. Not quite a garage, but pretty close.

- Six months later: we had twenty-eight people in 2,000 square feet of office space. We took over part of the second floor in the same building.

- End of year one: we moved our forty-eight people into a five-story building in the same office complex. This building had 20,000 square feet of space on each floor. Obviously, our now 4,000 square feet took up only a small part of one floor, but we were growing.

- Second year: we'd grown to 100 people in 20,000 square feet, on one full floor in the building,

- Fourth year: there were 200 people in 40,000 square feet, on two floors in the building.

- Eighth year: the company had grown to 450 people in 110,000 square feet (which is about the size of a Manhattan city block or a typical six-story office building). We were in four buildings.

- Thirteenth year: 1,000 people in 230,000 square feet in six buildings in the same office complex, known as the Houston Energy Corridor.

Paul and I actually shared a ten-foot by twenty-foot office in the beginning. This was great for communication but eventually a little distracting, because of the intensity with which we both worked. I was on the phone constantly, pursuing leads for projects, and Paul had a steady stream of people in and out of the office, asking technical questions about current projects. That arrangement sufficed for a while, but after six months, Paul moved into an office in the middle of the project team.

As noted, at 230,000 square feet, we were spread out in six office buildings in the same office complex. Because our people were organized into project teams, they were spread across all six of those buildings. In other words, the manager who oversaw all the mechanical engineers could not simply walk down a hallway to see what each and every person in the department was doing. The manager had to physically get out of his or her office and travel to the various buildings where people were working with their current project team. This forced Management By Wandering Around (MBWA). And again, those engineers and staff would constantly be moving around, even changing buildings, as they completed one project and moved on to another.

"MORPHING" AN ORGANIZATION FOR MAXIMUM FLEXIBILITY AND EFFICIENCY

The constant movement and constant change in our organization eventually was given a name by our people: *morphing*. People started calling it this, in order to better explain how Mustang worked to new employees, as they came on board. New people were always trying to figure how our organization was run. Then, just when people thought they had figured out how things were organized, something changed and surprised them.

For example, although I was one of the company's co-founders, I was not a sit-behind-the-desk executive. I worked on projects, too, sometimes as a project manager, but just as often as a project engineer working under someone else who was managing that project. People were constantly changing the "hats" they wore to suit whatever was needed on a particular project and whatever matched their skill sets, experience, and availability. We had a *"best player plays"* mentality.

Morphing was the art of continual change in the organization, which allowed the matrix organization (co-located teams instead of silos) to be whatever our clients needed us to be. Mustang could look like a fifteen-person company doing small projects, or it could look like a world-class organization that could stand toe-to-toe technically with the big oil companies, all the while executing in a much leaner fashion than was expected. Our structure was determined more by the mix of project organizations than by anything else.

WE TAUGHT OUR PEOPLE THAT OUR COMPANY WAS ESSENTIALLY A LARGE *TEAM OF TEAMS*, WITH A NUMBER OF TASKS TO ACCOMPLISH.

The organizational structure was radically different and somewhat difficult for outsiders (both clients and new hires) to understand. I worked to "paint a picture" in people's minds of what we were trying to accomplish through stories. Many times, when I realized people were not getting a concept, I would regroup and go to "paint-by-numbers." Let's fill in all the blue spaces, then the yellow, etc. until the picture became clear. Once they understood, they could teach others in their own words.

We taught our people that our company was essentially a large *team of teams*, with a number of tasks to accomplish. The organization of each project team morphed – seamlessly – to match those tasks in the most efficient way we could devise. The morphing happened regularly as everyone moved to be on tasks that needed their expertise and/or were ready to be completed. The result of this continual shifting of resources was highly efficient productivity!

Morphing was also used to move someone to a new position. With no announcement, someone would be eased over to see if they could handle a new responsibility. If it was not working out, they could be eased back without losing a good person. Announcements seemed to create friction for no good reason, whereas morphing seemed frictionless.

KEEPING EVERYONE AND EVERYTHING MOVING: MUSTANG MOTION

That's another way to bust silos: keep everyone and everything moving. When people stay too long in a physical space, they tend to settle in—which may sound like a good thing to do but isn't really. People get entrenched when they stay in one place too long, they get set in their ways, they start defending their "turf," and then they stop thinking creatively about different ways to do things.

We believed that no one in any organization should feel that he or she has any "turf" to defend. At West Point, the cadets use the phrase "cooperate and graduate," because the system is so tough you cannot make it alone. If you want people to *collaborate* and *cooperate* and *work together* toward a common goal; they are more likely to do that if they're not settled in any one room, office, or location.

To prevent entrenchment from happening in our company, we moved people's offices *constantly.* Having people move their workspaces strengthened the feeling of "perpetual motion" at Mustang. We didn't want anyone to get "stuck" in a job or a project; we

NO ONE IN ANY ORGANIZATION SHOULD FEEL THAT HE OR SHE HAS ANY "TURF" TO DEFEND.

wanted to be constantly moving forward, finishing projects and moving on to the next one—just like the "job on the corner of the desk" that I described in chapter 1.

Every few weeks, the pictures and announcements in the break rooms and coffee bars were changed to visually change the environment and to generate enthusiasm. Marketing helped with fun pictures of past activities and announcements of upcoming events. This was part of their "internal-sales" activities to help us motivate and retain people by giving them good things to talk about. We wanted to spiral their attitude up at the coffee bar or break room or conference room, so they would have a positive attitude as they moved through the halls and interacted with other people.

Everything about our company reinforced this feeling of Mustang Motion. We had chosen the Mustang name because of the success of the famous car, as well as the power, stamina, and speed of a mustang horse. Our logo reinforced those ideals: the horse is not standing still; it is rearing up on one hoof, ready to take off and run at top speed—just like us! Even the script used for our company name is slanted, as though it's moving. Our people adapted the song "Loco-motion" ("Everybody's doing a brand-new dance now; come on, do the locomotion") and renamed it "Mustang Motion." Someone always made sure that song was played at all of our company celebrations and parties!

All these choices and all our efforts regarding Mustang Motion were intended to get people accustomed to change, so that they would accept it, embrace it, look forward to it, and laugh about it. People moved quickly from one project to another, because that was just the way things were done at Mustang. We moved offices, changed projects, brought in new people—with no problems, no big deal; all done without interrupting the flow of work. Everyone had to be comfortable with uncertainty and change, because our industry was by no means static. We *needed* to be able to change and adjust our people, systems, and execution methodologies to match the needs of our clients on a continuous basis.

• • •

The same is true of most industries and businesses: if your company or organization hasn't changed in months, years, decades, or *ever*, and you're still successful, you are very unique. Think about it: if you're at least fifty years old in 2020, you started working before computers were ubiquitous, since the first "personal computer" came on the market in the early 1980s. If you're in your forties, you started working before there was email, which began to be used widely in the mid-1990s. The first mobile email device was the Blackberry, which came out in 1999, and Apple introduced the first smartphone in 2007, which means that anyone younger than twenty-five in 2020 hardly remembers what life was like before smartphones. That's an astonishing amount of technological change in only thirty-five years.

All that change affects many aspects of our lives. The way we work, manage, lead, sell, market, manufacture, travel, communicate, stay in touch, pay bills, and do everything else is constantly changing. To keep up with that, you need to find a way to *morph* your own organization so that you can continue to be adaptable to the changing needs of *your* clients, customers, vendors, and employees.

At the same time, to keep up with change in the outside world, you may also need to change the way you *manage* your internal organization. Which brings us to the next topic: managing differently to prevent silos from forming in the first place.

TURNING THE TRADITIONAL ORGANIZATIONAL PYRAMID UPSIDE DOWN

Most organizations are structured around the traditional top-down pyramid: the owners or top managers (the C-suite) are at the top, then there's a larger layer of senior managers, followed by an even larger layer of middle managers, and all the other "worker bees" are at the bottom of the pyramid. But that doesn't mean they have to operate that way.

We turned the traditional organizational pyramid upside down and simplified it. We did this from the start of our company, when it was just the three cofounders (with the support of a lawyer, a CPA, and an insurance provider on an as-needed basis). Each of us had one leg of an upside-down triangle, diagrammed on the next page:

We created our organization this way from the start to ensure administration and sales "supported" operations both visually and in actuality. Operations would concentrate on delivering our value proposition internally to our company and externally to our clients. We believed in being servant leaders to support our people, vendors, and clients.

This organization enabled each of us to work in our area of strength, while at the same time helping one another in running the business. We wanted to keep each side of the triangle streamlined and very supportive of project requirements. When the company was still just the three of us, we were each primarily responsible for one of the sides of the triangle. Paul headed the operations side, with primary responsibility for organizational development, hiring, and execution excellence in projects. Felix headed the administration side, with responsibility for invoicing, contracts, insurance, bills, and keeping us financially healthy. I headed the sales side, focusing on sales, marketing, and providing continuous work.

Although we believed that the person handling each side was the best in the industry, we also wanted to do anything we could to ease one another's load. The overlaps at the apexes of this equilateral triangle made us very strong, because it allowed us to know what was happening in the other two sides of the organization.

Even though our company expanded from the three of us to many thousands of people over time, the upside-down triangle didn't change. At Mustang, the owners were on the bottom, supporting the engineers and administrative staff with whatever they needed: tools, people, work, and encouragement. In turn, engineers and administrative staff supported the designers and administrative assistants, giving them everything they needed to be successful. Finally, the designers and administrative assistants put out the final product that supported the industry needs. Here's what our upside-down triangle looked like; see if it can work in *your* organization:

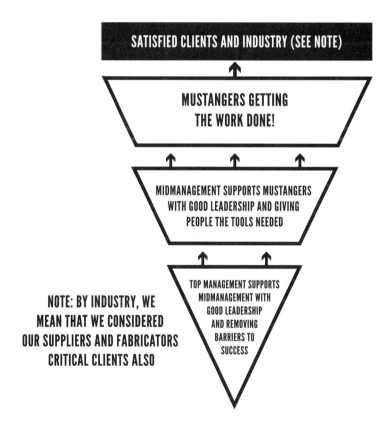

Even our offices were physically set up this way, with the owners on the first floor and the designers on the sixth floor with the nice views!

USING A MATRIX ORGANIZATIONAL STRUCTURE TO MANAGE WITHOUT SILOS

By our fourth year, we employed around 120 people, and we were increasing our head count rapidly. In fact, before we knew it, we had 200 people and were soon approaching 250. We thought it might be helpful to attend a few organizational-management seminars to learn more about how to manage a larger company; 120 people had been the traditional "glass ceiling" for companies in our industry. When companies hit that number, they stalled and then bounced between eighty and 120. How to be successful above that number was the burning question.

However, when we described how we worked (the matrix with people co-located on teams, the morphing to grow people, the perpetual motion, the reorganizing, and all the other practices that made our company so efficient) to the instructors at these seminars, they said our methods sounded like "complete chaos."

The management experts agreed that most start-up companies *require* their people to wear lots of hats and to be flexible about doing many different functions. But they also strongly felt that once a company grew beyond about twenty people, the organization needed to gravitate into silos, in order to manage growth and profit in each of the company's main areas.

Needless to say, after hearing this a few times, we gave up on the management seminars. It seemed that these "gurus" couldn't help us, because we had created an entirely different management structure. It had worked well for us as we grew from three people to thirty and then to 300. We just needed to make sure it continued to work all the way to 3,000 people and beyond! We didn't want to add any more layers of management than were absolutely necessary to stay in control of the Mustang Motion.

Looking back, I think the "matrix" organizational structure was not widely used at that time. In the book *American Icon*, Alan Mulally describes how he moved Ford Motor Company to a matrix organization between 2008 and 2015 in order to save the company. Reading this helped confirm the idea that companies could change their structure, even if they are one of the largest in the world. In our matrix organization, everyone had two bosses, as follows.

One boss is the *department manager.* In our company, that was someone to manage electrical engineers, or mechanical engineers, and so forth for each department. In your company, those department managers will be specific to *your* industry and your business. The department manager is typically responsible for all of the following:

- Hiring, firing, giving raises, and awarding bonuses to the people in his or her department.

- Keeping their people billable (gainfully employed).

- Staffing projects with people who have the technical knowledge and personality to support the project manager.

- Setting quarterly objectives for individuals.

- Developing more efficient ways of getting the job done and transferring that information to other projects.

- Cross-training and cross-fertilization of ideas.

To do all this, the department manager needs to understand the project workflow and then load and unload people to ensure that they have productive work to do on projects.

The other boss is the *project manager.* At Mustang, that was the person who managed perceptions and expectations of the client. The project manager is typically responsible for all of the following:

- Directing the day-to-day work of the people on the project team, to ensure that they accomplish the tasks they've been given, in concert with the rest of the team.

- Taking care of the client.

- Creating a bonded team culture.

- Insuring well planned and communicated handoffs between people and groups.

- Delivering value to the client in terms of cost, schedule, quality, and other critical success factors.

However, "delivering value to the project" did *not* mean that project managers were responsible for delivering a bottom-line profit to the company. Our project managers had *nothing* to do with profits. That approach is different from how many businesses manage their organizations. We wanted the project managers to be on the *same side of the table as the client*, not working *against* the client.

We also didn't want our company's invoices to be a source of conflict between our project manager and our client. By sitting on the same side of the table as the client, the project manager and the client could work together to figure out the absolute best way to deliver the project (in your case, maybe the end result of your initiative or task). Sometimes, this meant some of our scope of work went to vendors or competitors who had a different, but very efficient solution. In other situations, one of our engineers or designers might be physically located in a vendor's shop to help the vendor get the product completed on time.

Project managers could load and unload people to match the needs of the project.

Overall profitability was determined by the owners of our firm in the billing "Schedule of Rates." Then, in our matrix organization, the department managers were responsible for ensuring that the company met the overhead cost goals we had set. It was their responsibility to determine a person's billing rate and ensure their percent of billable hours met the targets.

BUSTING SILOS BETWEEN COMPANIES AND CLIENTS

Obviously, we did business differently from other firms in our industry. Our goal was to give our clients what they and their teams wanted, whether it was improved safety or easier maintenance or better first-year production, etc. To do that well, our clients needed to come in-house and integrate into our teams. In other words, we wanted to bust silos internally and also externally between us and our clients. We wanted to work together, in an inclusive manner, toward a common goal.

Having the client on our team enabled us to better control change, because the client knew what was involved in a change. Working with one another daily allowed us to feel comfortable in pushing back when the client requested a change that was not needed or was too late in the schedule. We would say "Let's put that on a list for the next project, because we need to stay the course and finish this one." *Controlling change was critical to success.*

This team spirit allowed us to control projects *much better* than companies that were walling themselves off from their clients. When they got through construction and startup, the companies that walled off communication with their clients would find that their clients were not totally satisfied with the end result, because it just didn't meet everything they had wanted. When we finished a project with close client collaboration, clients were very satisfied with the quality due to the ongoing communication and sense of teamwork. We simply had a different philosophy about including our clients and vendors: we wanted to bust silos everywhere we found them!

BE CAREFUL WHEN INCORPORATING ACQUISITIONS

One challenge of a tight-knit matrix culture is the same as in a silo organization. When an acquired company or team is introduced, they tend to stick together and become a silo because they are comfortable with each other and are still learning about how their new company operates. Your management team needs to be sensitive to this and work to break down the barriers that are inherent as soon as possible. One way is to instill a "blue layer" in the acquired unit, similar to how we busted unavoidable silos within Mustang.

Even with our focus on silo busting, we still had unavoidable ones. For example, each project team, while cross-functional, was a silo unto itself. HR and accounting and other groups had to be together, and each was essentially a silo. Some discussion across silos occurred with our outside activities, but we needed a more disciplined approach to ensure that "best practices" were being shared between these unavoidable silos. Luckily, we had some groups that worked across these silos, and they could be charged with the cross-training we needed.

The project-controls people doing cost and scheduling comprised one such functional group, design was another, and top management (COO, CFO, Strategic Planning, VP Sales, etc.) was a third. These groups comprised what we called the "blue layer" (based on our pervasive Mustang-blue color scheme) that could cross-communicate good ideas and ensure that efforts were not being duplicated across the various teams. This was critical in a fast-moving organization that was also changing rapidly.

The blue layer was also implemented on major projects. For example, Greg Sills was the project manager for BP on the "Atlantis" deep-water project. This would be a floating city in more than 7,000 feet of water 150 miles south of New Orleans. Production capacity would be 200,000 barrels of oil per day and 180 million cubic feet of natural gas. Atlantis would be a huge, world-class facility with a deck the size of two regulation soccer fields.

Greg knew that our teams communicated well and were always trying to make heroes of the companies we interacted with. He had us put a blue layer of Mustang people down in each area/silo on the project—for example, the subsea wellheads, the risers from wellheads to the hull, the hull, the drilling rigs, the processing facilities, and the quarters building. The blue layer people would identify possible cost savings if we could coordinate designs between silos. We could identify these by knowing the details of what was being worked on in each group and what their design restrictions were.

Then we would bring up those possible savings to the management team at monthly meetings. At one meeting, there was a possible $20 million savings if the design criteria between the risers and the hull were negotiated. Greg was then able to direct the heads of those silos to have their people get together across the silos and negotiate the design criteria to realize the savings. Without the blue layer, these savings would not have been identified in time for action.

This is important, as these savings had to be identified and worked in real-time or the opportunity (and the money) would be lost. This is the same whether you work in Bank of America or Foot Locker, or my son's business, Fab Fours. Having a blue layer where silos are unavoidable is the only way to get the communication required to operate efficiently.

OBJECTIVE:

Break the code on silo busting to become a Culture Code Champion. The reduced rework and savings identified will lower stress on your people and increase your bottom line.

BUST SILOS: GET EVERYONE WORKING TOGETHER

KEY POINTS TO KEEP IN MIND ABOUT BUSTING SILOS:

1. Be aware of problems caused by people working in silos: *rework ("do-overs"); elitism ("Why do they have bigger offices?"); competition instead of collaboration among departments; "unobtainium"—things that aren't possible to buy or build in the real world but are dreamed up by people who don't communicate with each other; and blame ("the dunce syndrome").*

2. "Co-locate" teams of people working together on projects, *instead of locating people by function, which actually separates people and reduces efficiency and productivity. If you've hired flexible people, they'll be happy to move around to work where they're most needed.*

3. "Morph" your organization, to accommodate project or task needs. *Talented people have many skills and a breadth of experience, so let them wear as many hats as they can and do whatever is needed on each new project.*

4. Keep everyone moving, so they don't get entrenched. *After all, you can't have "turf wars" if everyone shares the turf! Keep changing the environment as part of "internal sales" to spiral attitudes up. It all starts at the coffee bar: Do you post government regulations here or fun pictures of company events and volunteer activities?*

5. Manage differently. Ditch the traditional top-down pyramid approach *to management, where the "top" managers are "above" the next layer of managers, who are "over" the next layer of people. Instead, create servant leaders who support their people, vendors, and clients.*

6. Try the matrix approach to management, *where everyone reports to a project manager (who changes with each new project) as well as a department manager. Remember, this creates greater flexibility, and the more flexible your organization is, the more productive and successful it will be. This totally busts silos.*

7. Don't shut out your clients; invite them in! *The worst silos are the traditional barriers between an organization and its customers, which can create the dreaded "us vs. them" mentality. When you truly work with your clients, the work goes more smoothly. Successful projects lead to repeat business: happy clients, happy companies.*

8. Pay close attention to acquisitions of companies or teams. *They will automatically come in as silos, even if only temporarily for comfort in a new environment. Connect them into many areas of your company to break up their monolithic form.*

9. Add your own blue layer into unavoidable silos *to foster cross-communication between silos. If one team has a great idea for improved efficiency, you should share the idea to everyone in every team in your company immediately.*

Note: There isn't a chapter covering Step 4: Use Hard Copy Communication because it would be very short. This step is critical, however, for communication in developing your culture. Hard copy is mentioned throughout this book and includes such things as:

Planner Pad®
Swag/goodies
Newsletters
Miller Heiman sales Bluesheet®
Checklists
Oz Accountability® Pamphlet
Vision/values
Cost effectiveness list (lessons learned)
Signs in the garage and stairwells
Coffee bar postings
Signs and pictures on hallway walls and in conference rooms

CULTURE CODE CHAMPIONS WORKSHEET:
STEP 4: USE HARD COPY COMMUNICATIONS

STRENGTH:
Internal:_____

_____

WEAKNESS:
Internal:_____

_____

OPPORTUNITY:
External:_____

_____

THREAT:
External:_____

_____

CHAMPION:
Hand Step 4 baton to: _____

     Buddy: _____

Conceptual initial actions:

     1. _____

     2. _____

     3. _____

     4. _____

Start Date: _____

CHAPTER 5

COMMUNICATE: OPEN UP THE COMMUNICATION

I n every organization there are many handoffs between groups—not only externally between your company and your vendors and clients, but also internally. Every one of those handoffs can cause problems because of the lack of communication, miscommunications, or simple misunderstandings that can have complicated and serious (even disastrous) results. Over the years, we came to realize that *all problems are communication problems.* So, you need to do everything you can to improve the way everyone communicates with one another.

We've all been in situations where someone asks or tells you to do something; you think you understand; you do what you thought the person wanted; but when it's done, it's not right. When you both review what happened, you realize there was a communication breakdown at the outset. How often have you heard, "This isn't what

I meant at all!" This "someone" could be your boss, a co-worker, a supplier, your spouse, a client, a friend, or anyone.

Rework and revisions create enormous waste and inefficiency. This chapter offers some advice on how to improve communication throughout your organization: by fostering more and better interactions between people, by improving the handoffs from one group to another, and by cross-training people and sharing information. The goal is to *get things right the first time.*

PROJECT TEAMS: INCLUDE EVERYONE INVOLVED

The most important way to improve execution and efficiency is to foster and maintain a spirit of inclusion, with *everyone* who has any contact at all with a particular project. That means not only the core project team, but also *everyone* who contributes in any way.

Our focus on inclusion was not limited only to our in-house people, either. We also believed in the importance of our vendors and our clients, and we wanted them to be part of the team. I talked a little about pulling clients in on your team at the end of chapter 4, on silo busting. Our teams wanted to do the same thing with vendors.

Many companies treat their vendors very poorly: they seem to look down on the vendors, and they don't interact with them in a professional manner. Often, they tend to squeeze their vendors, in order to get the lowest price for the equipment or services that the vendors are bidding on.

One of the worst examples of this treatment that we heard about involved a large company that invited four vendors that were competing on a project to come in for an interview. Then they put each representative in a different room in the same hallway. The buyers moved from room to room, working to get concessions from each vendor. It was almost like a reverse-bid process: they asked each one, "Well, this other vendor said they would do such and such, so what will you do for us?" Interactions like these just seemed mean-spirited and unprofessional to us. Instead of doing a better job of defining a project so they could get a vendor's best price the first time, they put out a loose design, so they could squeeze their vendors during the bid-evaluation process.

The result of that squeezing is that the vendor, who is awarded the bid, is not happy at all. The vendor isn't sure if they're going to make any money, because they agreed to so many concessions, without enough time to work on the bid and really figure out what made economic sense. The vendor was under the gun, but they needed the work, so they agreed to whatever they were bullied into. In an interaction and a relationship like that, if you're the bully, you've set up a total win-lose situation, and the vendor is trying to protect itself. Even if it doesn't make any money on the project, the vendor hopes it won't *lose* money.

In contrast to other firms, our vendors were treated as an integral part of our team. Our bids for equipment showed the vendors where that equipment would go in the plant, how it would be hooked up, and what other equipment was around it. We wanted their brains turned on, because those vendors typically worked with fifty different engineering houses worldwide. That exposure meant they saw many different projects and configurations, and we wanted to get the benefit of any information and experience they had. If the vendor could bring that to our project and perhaps suggest a different configuration that would work better, then we could save our client money or reduce time in our client's schedule.

Even though engineers believe they are the experts, the vendors really are the topical experts for their equipment. In some situations, and on some projects, we actually trusted the vendor's expertise more than our own engineers because they competed every day on that equipment. By giving vendors all the available information, they could help us develop the best proven solution. Providing this additional information about the project before they bid on it benefited the vendors, as they often came up with a better solution that they could put in their bid. Sometimes that solution would differentiate them enough to win.

Once they won a bid, the vendor continued to be treated like they were part of the team, as though they were part of our company, delivering the project to our client. As a matter of fact, we made it a point to praise them in front of our clients to encourage clients to work with those vendors again.

USE VENDORS TO HELP SOLVE PROBLEMS

For example, we brought in one of our vendors on a heater-treater project for British Petroleum (BP), destined for an oil platform in the Gulf of Mexico. A heater treater is a vessel that uses heat to break down oil-water emulsions so that the oil can be accepted into a pipeline or some other method of transportation.

The scope of that project increased after we had started it, because BP (British Petroleum) was still drilling wells. That's the challenge with offshore work: no one knows exactly what's down there, so BP was drilling exploratory wells. Partway into the project, another well came in, which changed the equipment we needed to have on the platform in order to produce the reservoir.

There wasn't space for the new size of the oil heater treater that we needed once the project scope expanded. It was an eighty-foot-long vessel that was twelve feet in diameter. But we had already awarded the treater design and fabrication. We met with the vendor and showed them our restrictions due to the deck design. There were diagonals in the way due to the critical structural deck supports. The vendor came up with a way to split the same heater-treater system we had intended to use into three separate pieces that would fit in the space available. Because of the vendor's idea and the new configuration, we were able to shoehorn it into the deck that was already fabricated.

Working with our vendor enabled us to solve the problem in less than a week, which was an astonishingly short amount of time. If we had been working in the typical win-lose situation with both our client and the vendor, we would have had to shut down everything in that area for three months while we figured out how to solve the problem, and what it would cost.

Instead, we worked with the vendor *as a team,* and then we showed the solution to BP. We made the BP project manager a hero by solving the problem quickly without major changes to the existing deck or equipment cost and schedule.

Although we essentially added a few more pieces of equipment and changed some configurations, we were able to redo the engineering for the rest of the platform in less than two weeks and feed it to the fabrication yard with no schedule slippage. The vendor was able to make the change on the run, so that didn't change the vendor's schedule at all. Moreover, because there wasn't a significant delay, BP avoided the hazardous situation of having to install the deck during hurricane season, which is what would have happened if we had to shut down for three months. Because the vendor was involved in what was going on from the start, when the big change came through, they understood the whole project in detail and could quickly offer a good solution. That project was win-win-win for all of us, because we had open relationships with our vendor, the fabrication yard, and our client.

BRING CLIENTS IN AS PART OF THE TEAM

We were always very inclusive with all our clients. Again, as mentioned at the end of chapter 4 on silo busting, most companies kept their clients at arms' length away from the project team, because they didn't want the client saying, *hey I like this,* or *I prefer that*—and then changing the project a little bit. Those firms typically allowed only their top management to talk to clients; anybody below top management never saw or interacted with clients at all.

In contrast, our clients had space in our offices. Our clients knew our administrative assistants; they knew our designers; they knew the purchasing people who were working on their projects. Over time, our clients asked for people by name to work on their projects.

Having a client ask for someone by name to work on the next project was *hugely motivating* to our people. When a designer was told, "Hey, Mobil is coming back in with a new project, and they've requested you," the designer was not only flattered to be singled out but also motivated to finish up whatever project he or she was working on. They wanted to be available when the client needed them. That's another way to implement the "job on the corner of the desk" that was described in chapter 1. When you have work waiting for you, you're more motivated to finish what you're currently working on so that you can move on to the next project.

All this interaction between our people, our clients, and our vendors helped us do work more efficiently and with higher quality. Our clients could feel the team pulling for them. Similarly, the people in our company felt they were working *with* the vendors and working *with* the clients to deliver the project. That cooperation became a much broader team culture than just within our company. It was cooperation on that project *across the entire industry.*

ADDING BRAINPOWER AND EXPERIENCE FROM THE COMPANIES YOU'RE WORKING WITH TYPICALLY IMPROVES THE PROCESS AND STREAMLINES THE PROJECT.

That's the level of cooperation and teamwork that *you* want to achieve in your organization. So, don't shut out your vendors, and don't shut out your clients because you're afraid they'll bog down your work. Usually, the opposite thing happens: adding brainpower and experience from the companies you're working with typically improves the process and streamlines the project—which can save time and money for everyone involved. Such inclusiveness truly is a win-win situation and makes heroes all around.

YOU DON'T KNOW WHAT YOU DON'T KNOW

I learned many of these team culture-building techniques in the army. I was an honor graduate of the Army Ranger School and "King of the Pits" (hand-to-hand combat training). With that training and notoriety, it seemed to me that leading a combat engineering platoon would be a snap. But my platoon met its match when tasked to put together a raft to transport vehicles across a river at Fort Hood, Texas. The battalion wanted to have a competition to see which platoon could build the raft fastest and with no safety issues. Over a six-week period, we were going to practice building it twice, then do it as a timed exercise.

The raft (as pictured above) would consist of rubber pontoons (each about the size of four pickup trucks, end to end), with M4T6 bridge components on top of them. M4T6 consisted of steel pieces that took one, two, or four men to carry. The steel pieces are put together with three-inch diameter pins that are "tapped" in with a hammer. All people over water had to wear life preservers for safety.

Although seemingly straightforward, it took us *five hours and twenty minutes* of sweat and cursing to get that thing together, when the army manual says an hour and a half is the standard! Out of twenty-two platoons in the battalion, only four of them beat five hours, and two platoons did it in less than four hours.

We had lots of excuses: our air compressor broke, some of the steel pieces were bent, the life preservers made it hard to move, it took full swings with a sledgehammer to get some pins in, etc., etc. We tried again two weeks later and brought our time down to four hours and fifteen minutes. One platoon was down close to three hours. We felt the improvement had come through familiarity with the task, changing out some of the bent steel pieces, and having put the raft together about thirty times.

But if the army standard is ninety minutes, it should be able to be done in sixty, since the standard has a lot of assumptions about weather and terrain. I took my guys over in the shade, still hot and tired from our latest effort, to brainstorm what we could do better, while everything was still fresh from our four-hour effort. This was similar to the hotwash exercise described in the *Black Hawk Down* preface to this book.

First, there was a lot of venting and complaining, but I persisted in asking them to think and started to get a list of problems people could identify. I felt that if I could get a hard copy list, we could discuss each item and come up with ideas to solve them. One really big guy said he had trouble moving around on the raft to pound in pins, because he was wearing a life preserver. Blowing up the pontoons took over an hour as guys were in knee-deep water, and getting to both sides of the pontoons was tough. The compressor, the weight of the pieces, etc. were all brought up, until we had about thirty obstacles to our success. Then we started talking about solutions.

You could have knocked me over with a feather when a buck sergeant said that when they did these bridge sections in Germany, they laid the pins out on plywood and brushed used motor oil on them to make them slip into the steel pieces easier. This showed me that you don't know what you don't know until there is a reason to find out. We went over and tried oiling a pin, and it went in with a small hammer! This meant that we could take the big guys off of the raft and use them to manhandle the big pieces up onto the raft, checking off about four of our obstacles.

Our scoop loader operator, a young private with two years in the army, had the task of lifting the rolled-up pontoons off the dump truck and taking them close to the water. He said that if we inflated them on land, he could push them into the water with his scoop, without damage. This was a brilliant idea! Remember ... value all levels in your organization. Now we were building momentum to spur more ideas. We decided to rig up two hoses from the air compressor and replace the fuse with a nail ... not recommended, but our compressor was finicky.

We listed the steel pieces in the order we needed them and decided which team (half a squad) would get each one. We decided who would be up on the raft and listed it all out in detail. By the time we were done planning and brainstorming, we had a solution to every obstacle on the list plus the new ones we came up with during the discussion.

Two weeks later, we were out in the field getting ready for the real raft competition and had a finely tuned plan. In the middle of the night, my platoon sergeant woke me up and said I was having a nightmare yelling "Swing that hammer!" We would be the eighth platoon to compete and already two platoons had done the raft in just under two hours.

When the gun went off, we were crazy good. One hundred percent focused action. People had what they were doing, in order, written on their hands, and they knew when to help someone else stay on track. Everyone knew the big picture as well as the detail of his individual part. It was a dead sprint, and we couldn't believe it when our time was announced as forty-eight minutes! The platoon picked me up, carried me to the end of the raft, and threw me in the river. We were unbelievably excited about this success, and you can just imagine what a bonded team we had become!

We had the energy and enthusiasm that I had come to believe is a force multiplier, in military terms. We had a good plan, and we had the esprit to take care of each other. All of this, working together under good leadership at all levels, accomplished something that would have been a "way-out-there" goal, if it had been envisioned when we started two months earlier.

The answers to efficiency are in your organization: you just have to encourage people to speak up with what they know and then act. The "how-to" is there, and then, with good leadership, you can smooth out the handoffs to create high-performing teams.

PREVENT AND AVOID MISCOMMUNICATION

Over time, we had several situations where an engineer or designer or purchasing person or fabrication inspector messed up, due to poor communication or lack of understanding. Everything would be touched multiple times through the course of a project. Our teams believed strongly in the phrase *"don't expect what you don't inspect."* We worked hard to cross-train all these people's knowledge to ensure that "all eyes are informed eyes." We wanted them to catch each other's mistakes when they did their part. Early on, we found out that in many cases, people would not speak up when they saw something that did not seem right.

Why didn't they? I believe these problems happen because a designer, for example, might notice something seems wrong, but he or she isn't comfortable challenging the engineer by asking about it. This might have happened anywhere (or even everywhere) down the line. In

WE WORKED HARD TO FOSTER AN ORGANIZATION-WIDE CULTURE WHERE IF YOU SAW SOMETHING AND IT DIDN'T LOOK RIGHT, YOU WOULD FEEL COMFORTABLE CHALLENGING IT, NO MATTER WHO YOU WERE OR WHO YOU WERE CHALLENGING.

order to prevent this miscommunication and/or lack of communication between groups, we worked hard to foster an organization-wide culture where if you saw something and it didn't look right, you would feel comfortable challenging it, no matter who you were or who you were challenging. We didn't want anyone to be afraid or embarrassed, because we needed to get things right.

This approach was instituted from the start of our company, because there were some very strong-willed engineers who were rather imposing and very vocal. We saw that some of the people they worked with, in other departments, were afraid to speak up and challenge them. They thought it wasn't "appropriate" for them to question the engineers, but when we saw what was happening, we took a zero-tolerance stance: if an engineer wasn't open to questions, they were encouraged to leave and find work elsewhere.

That ties in to the culture of our organization. Suffice it to say that we worked hard to create an environment where all our people really got to know each other, *enjoyed* working together, and felt comfortable asking questions, so that there were no barriers to doing the best possible work. I'm sure that whatever your organization does, there have been communication breakdowns between people that have led to some very amusing or possibly very serious mistakes. Don't let that happen. Remember, *all* problems are *communication* problems, so if you foster better communication in your organization, your people will be more productive, more efficient, and happier.

SQUEEZE HANDOFFS TO AVOID WASTING TIME BETWEEN PROJECT TASKS

Hundreds of handoffs happen every day in organizations, unless people are working completely alone on a project or task. Since that isn't the situation in most organizations, handoffs become problems very easily.

Whenever I hear the term handoff, I picture an Olympic relay race. If the first runner is running at full speed and is ready to hand off the baton, but the next runner is not up to speed, that's going to be a difficult, awkward and slow handoff.

Similarly, if your team has the slowest runner coming in with the baton, then the second runner who is waiting for the handoff is wasting time. Standing around waiting is not the way to win a race, and it's not an efficient way to work, either. The handoff from one task to the next or one phase of a project to the next requires good accountability from both sides of the handoff.

On all projects or initiatives or tasks worked on in the company, we tried to ensure that anyone who would be handing off something to another person would start a conversation early. With that approach, people could hand off their task in a format that would be immediately usable by the other person. The early talking about formats and quality allowed each person to get the task right the first time and prevent rework.

Each person needs to commit to when he or she will deliver work and then has to be accountable to that date. Also, the next person needs to be ready on that date to use what is delivered. In too many organizations, when one person or group actually meets the date that was promised, the next group is surprised. The people in that next group are like the runner who is standing around waiting, instead of starting to run so the handoff can be smooth. I've actually heard people say, "Oh, no! You actually delivered it when you said you would. We didn't think that would happen, so we won't be ready for you for another three weeks."

When this happens, all that time is wasted. To prevent that from happening, our teams worked both sides of every handoff, so they would be very seamless. We started doing this on small projects, but it became even more important when large, world-class projects came in. Those projects had schedules with thousands of lines, so our people reviewed them carefully to find where the key handoffs were. For example, a 3,000-line-item schedule might have forty-five critical handoffs. If you focus on making those handoffs seamless, you can save 25–30 percent in that project's schedule. That is where we built a differentiated reputation, with a repeatable process, and you can, too.

We also improved handoffs of work we did with our partners on some projects. Sometimes that caused us to change the way we did things (since, obviously, you can't change the way someone else or another company does things). For example, in 2002, we were working on the Northstar project for British Petroleum Alaska (BPA). It was the first offshore oil production in the world located north of the arctic circle.

While reviewing how the contractors in Alaska were going to do their piping, they told us they would redo our piping drawings into a software package called Acorn. They did that because Acorn generated all the details and bar codes they needed to make the pieces of pipe and track them through fabrication. Using Acorn was a benefit to the contractors, but having them redo our drawings was a waste of time.

We bought the Acorn software and spent a day in training, to learn how to use it. Then all our drawings were done in the fabricator's formats, with the Acorn software. This saved them from having to hire piping designers, reduced errors from their re-drawing efforts, and delivered materials to their yards twelve weeks earlier. Those benefits resulted in significant project savings, and we named this new design method a "Digital and Digestible" handoff. There was "free money" available to the project just from us squeezing this handoff. We sub-optimized our design work, because Acorn was not as efficient for us to use, but that was a small price to pay for the gains in schedule and quality for BPA. Essentially, we put ourselves in the shoes of the fabricator's people and figured out how to best serve them in the handoff.

Our methods helped strip all the fat out of doing projects by working the handoffs between design, purchasing, and construction. This next statement is critical. *We built our company from squeezing handoffs everywhere.* There is "free money" as shown above, available in handoffs that we saved for our clients and vendors.

By the way, you might think we were tempted to just keep that "free money" as a reward of our innovative thinking. However, due to our core cultural values, open communication and reimbursable contracting, we never did. We were always working to build trust bridges throughout the industry.

CROSS-TRAIN PEOPLE AND SHARE INFORMATION

In addition to developing a culture where people communicate more effectively and share information more freely, the example in the previous section also introduces another important way that organizations can improve their overall efficiency and productivity: cross-training. As mentioned, we believed that all eyes should be informed eyes, and the way to make that happen is to train your people so that they're more knowledgeable about their own work—and become more educated about other people's work and responsibilities.

I realize that some people reading this may be rolling their eyes or groaning because they think, "We're so busy just training our people to do their *own* jobs; where are we going to find the time and resources to cross-train them to learn how to do *other people's jobs?*"

First, let's look at the benefits of cross-training, and then I'll describe the logistics, so you'll see how easy it can be.

You want to get your people to broaden their knowledge and expand the scope of what they normally do in their own jobs. For example, the primary responsibility of a purchasing agent is to take specifications and drawings for a piece of equipment, bid it out, and get bids in from a variety of vendors. Then the engineer will evaluate those bids. But we wanted our purchasing people to do more. We wanted them to study those bid documents and ask the engineers questions, so they could begin to fully understand what they were sending out for bids. When that happened, they became about 60–70 percent as good as the engineers in reviewing the bid documents to make sure they were accurate and complete before being sent out to vendors. Also, when the vendors had questions, those purchasing agents were knowledgeable enough to answer many more of the commonly asked questions, without having to involve the engineers. This saved time and cost for the client, because purchasing people cost less and there was no handoff to engineering.

The end result was that our designers knew the specifications on a piece of equipment, our engineers knew that piece of equipment, and our purchasing agents knew that piece of equipment as well. So, throughout the entire bid-award cycle—i.e., from vendor data review to inspection—we had many more people who understood the details of what we were trying to get for that piece of equipment. And when *all eyes are informed eyes,* we were able to catch things that might not have been caught until after they were built, or even after they were installed.

Okay, so that's the benefit: preventing mistakes, improving accuracy, saving time and money. Now, how do you find time to cross-train? In our company, we used whatever downtime occurred, so that no one was ever sitting around waiting for the next project to come in. For example, if an instrument engineer got slow, and there was no more instrument work for that person to do, then he or she moved over to automation or to some other functional area that was related to his or her regular job but slightly different. While that person might be a senior-level instrument engineer, he or she would work in a midlevel capacity in the new area, learning from the senior-level people—but would still be doing real work on real projects, working with experienced people and could get up to speed very quickly in the new area. Then that person would return to instrument engineering, either when a project came in or when the senior-level people felt they were up to speed in the new discipline.

This was done in all departments, including HR, sales, marketing, legal, and strategic planning, whenever work slowed down.

Again, I realize there may be skeptics reading this who might say, "We don't have any downtime, and there aren't any slow times. Our business is not cyclical, and everyone in our organization is busy (and overworked) every minute of every day." Frankly, I have real trouble believing there are companies or organizations out there that don't have *any* downtime. On the other hand, I *do* believe there are people in many organizations that do what we call "making eight"— which means they make themselves look busy for eight hours a day, when they really aren't.

However, if you really don't have any downtime or slow periods, I recommend you actually *schedule time for cross-training your people.* This is easy to organize into a matrix. Figure out who you need to cross-train and find the areas of your business where cross-training will pay off the most. In a very short amount of time, I'm confident you'll start saving money on the handoffs from one department to the next, because your people will be more knowledgeable about the next person's area of expertise.

• • •

Another way to find time for cross-training is through "lunch-and-learns." Everybody eats lunch or at least takes a break at mid-day, and food is a great way to lure people to get together. We started having lunch-and-learns pretty much from the very beginning of our company. Each one was about an hour to an hour and a half, and most departments had a lunch-and-learn meeting at least once a month.

During the first six years of our company, about fifteen to twenty-five people attended each one. Later on, when the size of our company—and our office space—had increased considerably, we moved them to larger training centers, which could accommodate forty to fifty people.

Typically, purchasing invited vendors to come in and talk to us about their products and services. They were happy to oblige, because vendors are always looking for ways to connect with their customers, and the cost of bringing in some sandwiches and soft drinks was nothing, considering the exposure they would gain with our employees. The lunch-and-learns were also a great way for us to develop better relationships with our vendors. We had lunch-and-learns on control panels, on platform cranes, on insurance, on reviewing contracts, just about anything related to our business.

For example, we had a lunch and learn on electrical equipment, hosted by one of our vendors in that area. In addition to purchasing, the groups attending were electrical designers and electrical engineers, as well as some people from instrumentation and automation who wanted to learn more about the electrical side. The vendor's sales team talked for fifteen to twenty minutes about their equipment, how it was different from other vendors' equipment, and the pros and cons of using it. The vendors usually brought brochures or other information that they distributed, and they also exchanged contact information.

The rest of the time in the lunch-and-learn was used to talk about what improvements we could make in our design process. Electrical team members from different projects started talking about what they were working on, and typically, someone would solicit ideas from the group on how to do things more efficiently and expeditiously. Since some automation and the instrument people were there, too, they had the opportunity (which they wouldn't have had otherwise) to hear those discussions among the electrical team and what they were trying to do. They started to get a feel for that aspect of the project—in other words, cross-training was happening.

These gatherings brought together people who normally didn't interact. In this case, automation and instrument people met their counterparts from the electrical department, and got to know them. Later on, when they were working on something and needed input from electrical, they knew who they could call. In many large organizations with hundreds or thousands of employees, that type of interaction may never happen. When people don't know someone to call for their expertise, they're going to just muddle through and do the best they can on their own. The lunch-and-learns were a great way to introduce people to other departments, to expose and train them in other aspects of the business, and to learn more and develop stronger relationships with our vendors. All this was done over lunch, which made it easy to schedule.

What can you learn from other projects and other teams in *your* organization?

OBJECTIVE:

Break the code on better communication and handoffs to become a Culture Code Champion. The reduction in errors and increased efficiency will help your people make heroes of each other and flow right to your bottom line.

COMMUNICATE: OPEN UP COMMUNICATION

KEY POINTS TO KEEP IN MIND ABOUT COMMUNICATION:

1. All problems are communication problems. *Analyze any problem, and the root cause is a miscommunication—or the complete lack of communication on some aspect of the task. Do everything you can to improve the lines of communication between everyone, inside and outside your organization.*

2. Include everyone as part of the team. *That applies not only to everyone in your organization but also your vendors and clients. Creating this type of teamwork facilitates communication so there are no unpleasant surprises later on down the line. The goal is to get things right the first time.*

3. You don't know what you don't know. *The answers to efficiency improvement and waste reduction are probably in your organization; just ask your people.*

4. Make "all eyes informed eyes," *and empower your people to speak up if they see a problem. A corollary is "don't expect what you don't inspect." Get everyone helping.*

5. Squeeze handoffs everywhere. *There is "free money" available in handoffs. Make sure no one (and no department or company) is standing around waiting for a handoff, and your project schedules will reduce dramatically. A 30 percent reduction in cost and schedule is available.*

6. Cross-train your people so they'll better understand what others do. *When they don't, that's when work slows down, as though everyone on the team is speaking a different language.*

7. Implement a "lunch-and-learn" program. *Bring in vendors or other experts to educate your team on new technologies, new equipment, or new methods of working. Schedule these sessions over lunchtime, because everyone should take a midday break, and good food lures even the most reluctant participants! We called these "lunch-and-learns" and we held them about once a month. We always had a terrific turnout.*

CULTURE CODE CHAMPIONS WORKSHEET:
STEP 1: OPEN UP THE COMMUNICATION

STRENGTH:
Internal:_____

_____

WEAKNESS:
Internal:_____

_____

OPPORTUNITY:
External:_____

_____

THREAT:
External:_____

_____

CHAMPION:
Hand Step 1 baton to: _____

    Buddy: _____

Conceptual initial actions:

    1. _____

    2. _____

    3. _____

    4. _____

Start Date: _____

CHAPTER 6

EXECUTE: ESTABLISH A REPEATABLE PROCESS

aving a strong execution process for your work is critical in developing your culture. It will enhance communication, help with cross-training and deliver more sales. This will increase the value of your brand and help you bring in more top people. People are attracted to a winner ... your process is important!

Since our business started in a "bust" cycle in our industry, we constantly strove to *not* be beholden to that boom-and-bust cycle and be captive to it. Our goal was to be solid in good times and bad.

A few years later, we found the perfect motto to summarize our desire to avoid bust cycles. Although the source was unlikely, it didn't matter to us. Our inspiration came from the movie *Terminator 2: Judgment Day,* where Sarah Connor (played by Linda Hamilton) was determined that there would be "no fate but what we make for ourselves"; she even carved "NO FATE" into a picnic table.

Seeing that, we realized that was exactly what our goal had been all along. In believing that we didn't have to spiral up and down with the rest of the industry, we believed there was "No Fate" and we wanted to develop a No Fate leadership team. Don't let your organization get sucked into standard industry boom/bust cycles. The oil and gas industry was notorious for these, but every industry has cycles. Instead, you should determine *your own fate*. In this chapter, I'll show you how, with a good project execution process.

THE PROJECT INFLUENCE CURVE SHOWS WHERE YOU SHOULD PUT EMPHASIS

In the previous chapters, I've been discussing how to build a team culture across all phases of your business. We have covered hiring, developing your team culture, selling, and busting silos for better communication; now we want to ensure that your team can execute better than the competition. What we have addressed is applicable to HR, sales, marketing, operations like manufacturing, and new product development, all the way to legal and financial reporting. The culture, however, has to work hand in hand with good project discipline in order to deliver a successful company. Everything in business is a project, initiative, or task; ours were just more obvious.

About twelve years into my career, while sitting in an ARCO project manager's office, I was shown the following Project Influence Curve (I added the Cost Curve):

PROJECT INFLUENCE AND COST CURVES

The project influence curve shows that you have the greatest ability to affect project outcomes early in the project, when costs are smallest. The project cost, schedule, quality, safety, etc. can be most influenced during the conceptual phase when decisions are being made and the plan is being formed. Mustang became the best in the industry at this front-end planning effort. This concept is true for any HR initiative or marketing task or anything your people are doing. Front-end discipline makes a person or team keep the end in mind when they are setting up the task or project. They have to answer the question, "What are our desired outcomes?"

Although I'm a professional engineer and owned an engineering firm, I always told clients that "engineering is a necessary evil to get into purchasing and construction." That phrase made them sit up and listen! Construction is where the rubber meets the road, because the costs are the greatest and the team learns how good the design is. But how do you get there in good shape?

FINISH ONE PROJECT PHASE BEFORE MOVING TO THE NEXT

Most people are familiar with the term *work-breakdown structure,* where you break down a project or task into its component pieces. In the mid-1990s, big projects were getting out of control, so they broke them down into pieces, but there were too many pieces, the teams were too big, and projects were delivering poor results for clients.

Projects generally got out of control because the team continued to move forward through the design stage, through the purchasing stage, and into the construction stage, while several pieces of the work would still be back in the concept stage due to options still being considered. This often happened because the big oil companies had so many fingers in the pot (so to speak) that their decisions wouldn't stick. Obviously, once you're in the construction stage, installing equipment or putting down pipe, that's not a good time for decisions and plans to still be in the process of being firmed up and finalized. At that point, it costs big dollars to make changes, since the changes will impact equipment that has already been fabricated. That's where those project managers seemed to lose control of their costs and schedules. In reality, the poor results come from poor project discipline in earlier stages.

To solve this problem, many oil companies began implementing a new concept, called *Stage-Gate,* which was recommended by the benchmarking company they used. This approach used a work-breakdown structure, but it assigned specific tasks to different stages of a project. At each stage, there were certain tasks that needed to be completed and delivered to a gatekeeper. The gatekeepers usually had profit and loss responsibility, so they were keenly interested in cost, schedule, safety, and quality. Once the design was approved by the gatekeeper, a "design freeze" was declared. Once frozen, those project decisions and designs could not be changed unless the project was stopped, and everyone moved back to that stage. This was tough discipline, but it was needed for control. Once there was a design freeze, the team could move on to the next stage of the project.

This approach forced more discipline into projects and gave better results. All the major oil companies started implementing a Stage-Gate process, with varying degrees of success. They named their work process so their people would rally around it, learn it and use it. We did the same thing with our Pacesetter and Stagecoach project execution processes. *Name your process and brand it to differentiate.*

Stage-Gate was a great approach to project planning, so we embraced it, completely and thoroughly. Other firms did not embrace it, because they felt it was restrictive. In contrast, we believed "the plan will set you free." If we had a good plan and decisions that would stick, then we were free to make it happen for the client.

Using a work-breakdown structure was also a good way to actually help control construction costs.

Remember the BP client mentioned earlier, who wore a mop for hair and would wear it for a year for the $300 million we saved him on the Clair project? That savings was primarily generated from two things we typically did.

First, we did not start with a blank sheet of paper like the London team did. We had completed a project for Mobil Equatorial Guinea that closely matched all the design parameters of Clair. Instead of a go-by for just a piece of equipment, we used the entire equipment deck as the go-by with all the equipment. The go-by used an open deck design, which was common in the Gulf of Mexico but not for international work. We then challenged the BP team on anything they wanted to change for the North Sea. Since the

Mobil project was still in the fabrication yard, we took the BP people from London to Corpus Christi, Texas, and walked around on it for detailed discussions.

Secondly, we skid-mounted all the production equipment and split those skids out to twelve small fabrication shops all around the UK. These skids were our work-breakdown structure for the production facility. Normal practice was to build all the production facilities up on the deck, sixty feet in the air. We put thousands of components on small skids, resulting in thirty-five nice lifts up onto the deck and easy hookup to each other. This method used more engineering and some more steel for the skids, but it kept the schedule and cost tightly controlled. Each skid was a frozen piece of the design per the stage-gate philosophy and principles. *Can you do something similar with your work product and process?*

PLAN AHEAD: START WITH THE END IN MIND

Our teams took that approach of "eating the elephant one bite at a time" to the next level, by *starting with the end in mind.* This may sound obvious to some readers, but it's surprising how many project managers—even experienced ones—schedule projects forward instead of backward, as we did. When you start with the goal in mind, or the deadline, it's much easier to see what tasks or phases are sucking up the most time, or where the biggest problems will be.

For example, we did a project for British Gas where we would be putting the first ever platform offshore Tunisia, Africa. The typical way this project would be handled would be to have the equipment decks fully outfitted onshore and then transported with a lift barge to the installation location. This saves money, because work offshore is five times as expensive as doing it onshore. Unfortunately, there were no lift barges anywhere near Tunisia; they were all located in the North Sea (between Scotland and Norway) or in the Gulf of Mexico. Obviously, both those locations are very far from North Africa, so using lift barges from either location would necessitate an enormous mobilization cost. The problem was compounded by the fact that there was only one lift barge in each location that could lift the fully outfitted equipment deck. Lack of competition always made the price escalate due to the demand for that installation equipment.

So, while we were still planning the project, we looked at that problem and figured out how to split the deck into multiple pieces. This opened up the bid list to six smaller lift barges that could do the installation. That enabled us to dramatically reduce the mobilization cost from the Gulf of Mexico or the North Sea and not put our client in a bind if those two heavy-lift barges were unavailable. As it turned out, other complications arose on the project, so the lift barge was needed onsite for an extra twenty days—and having a smaller and less-expensive barge helped our client control costs.

Our approach to "starting with the end in mind" when we were doing the design benefited not only British Gas, it also benefited us— and other clients. We showed what we did to several of our clients, and that approach became a differentiator for us. These experiences showed clients that we weren't going to allow them to be boxed into a corner, especially at the end of a project, when costs can increase substantially. It all started with understanding the project influence curve and developing a good work-breakdown structure that allowed us to backward plan the project and squeeze the cost and schedule.

You can do the same thing where you work. Figure out what end results you want. Backward plan the sequence of activities to the start. Review the key handoffs, and determine what is needed on both sides for a smooth handoff so you can squeeze money and schedule at those points. You will be amazed at the resulting plan.

DON'T REINVENT THE WHEEL: BOX IN YOUR "ARTSY" PEOPLE

Another great way to improve your organization's execution and efficiency is to make sure you're not reinventing the wheel with every new project or task you take on. This happens in so many organizations, because no one wants to think they're doing rote tasks or working on an assembly line. Most people want to bring some creativity and intelligence to their work, so that it is satisfying and feels worthwhile.

Unfortunately, in almost every organization, no matter what you make or do, there are some people or groups who simply want to be *too* creative. They actually *do* want to reinvent the wheel, so that every project they work on is unique and special. But that's an incredibly inefficient way to work, and in most cases, it's not necessary. That's why, in our company, we worked diligently to "box in the artsy."

Our "artsy" people were our engineers. Typically, on every new project, engineers wanted to use their expertise by starting with a blank sheet of paper, thinking, *"Hmmm; what's this structure going to look like? What equipment am I going to use on this one?"* That approach drove us nuts; as self-proclaimed efficiency experts, we wanted to tell them, "Hey, the objective is to buy stuff and build stuff, so it can produce product for the client. That's all we need to do."

We wanted the KISS principle in everything that closely matched … Keep It Super Simple. For example, we believe in "three bids and a buy" to keep purchasing simple. Just imagine the savings over having 12 bids, an exhaustive bid evaluation and conditioning period and finally an award. Then you still need to communicate with the other

11 bidders on why they lost!

Similarly, our designers created drawings that seemed to change things from previous designs just so that they would be different. We often wondered if the designers were doing drawings that they wanted hung on the wall to be appreciated as gorgeous works of art. That also drove us nuts! We only needed those drawings so we could build what needed to be built; after that, the drawings could figuratively be thrown away. So, we wanted to find ways to box in our artsy engineers and designers, to stop them from designing one of a kind works of art. We wanted them to focus on doing only what was required, so we could move on to purchasing equipment, starting construction, and producing product for our clients.

You don't have to be in our industry to have artsy people: as mentioned, almost every organization has them. Maybe it's your lawyers, who want to draft a new contract for every situation, when a boilerplate is all they really need—at least as a starting point, for most negotiations. Maybe it's your finance people, who want to do a new analysis for every report you ask for—when they could simply modify something that's already working for another report. Even in the most creative types of work, there's always a way to use *something* that's been done before, even if you do adapt it to a new project. Think about how many times you've heard books or movies or recipes or works of art described as something similar but with a new twist. We liked to think of our process as "Bespoke with a manufacturing mentality." The designs were individualized and tailored (bespoke), but they were put together efficiently.

To improve efficiency, try to use whatever you can that's already been created—commonly called "go-bys." *Don't* reinvent the wheel; *use* the old wheel as a building block for your new project. In our company, as you know by now, we wanted to have a "job on the corner of the desk" for as many people as possible, and we wanted to keep things moving to finish projects so that our clients would be happy, and we could do even *more* work. Whenever possible, we re-used and recycled pieces of other projects as a starting point, tailoring them to the new requirements.

When awarded new projects, we would prepare for a kickoff meeting. This was a critical habit of ours—we *always* had a kickoff meeting. Our top people would gather together to look at our bid and the layout. Then they went into our libraries and pulled detailed vendor information for equipment that closely matched the requirements. Our goal was to have 30 percent of the project defined with go-bys at the kickoff meeting.

> *DON'T* REINVENT THE WHEEL; *USE* THE OLD WHEEL AS A BUILDING BLOCK FOR YOUR NEW PROJECT.

For example, if we were doing a project for Mobil, pieces were pulled from previous projects that we had done for Texaco, Conoco, Exxon, and BP. The team started with those pieces from the earlier projects to create the new design. Then, those go-bys were adapted to match Mobil's requirements. Generally, there would be some pieces the team did not have a go-by for due to the process requirements, or because of the way the client wanted to operate. These pieces would be done from scratch.

I know some readers may be thinking that some clients might object to this approach and say, "You can't do that with our project: you can't simply take one element from column A and another from column B; our project isn't an à la carte menu." Or, "We don't want you to just 'cut and paste' elements from projects you've done in the past, because what we're doing is so new, so cutting edge, so special, that nothing you have could apply to our project." Or, "We don't want a cookie-cutter design; we're hiring you to create something *from scratch*."

But that didn't happen, because our clients weren't that concerned with how we did our drawings or prepared their bid packages. They reviewed the drawings and bid packages only for compliance with their stated requirements. When we showed clients that the designs were based on proven past work, it actually boosted their trust in us. They didn't want one-of-a-kind prototypes, either, if they could get tried-and-true. This gave them contingency in cost and schedule for unforeseen events that always seem to crop up.

Continuing with the Mobil example, we created what we called "paper-doll layouts." During the planning phase of a project, we would cut out pieces of cardboard to scale for the size of the equipment go-bys. In this case, we might use three compressors from a Texaco project, to provide the outline for the paper-doll templates. The Texaco vendor information would show us exactly where all the connections were for piping, for electrical, and for control systems. The drawings would also show the weights for the structural design, and they provided a three-dimensional envelope to visualize the fit. This would definitely "box-in" the layout requirements.

When meeting with Mobil management, we would tell them we were planning to use a go-by and tweak it to their requirements. But the beauty of not reinventing the wheel is that, if we saw something in Mobil's specifications that would cost significantly more or would wreck the schedule, we could bring that to their attention with these layouts and go-bys. Generally, the client would authorize the specification change to reduce cost or help the schedule.

That is how we "boxed in the artsy" people as often as possible. We weren't averse to trying new things, but we weren't going to do that at a client's expense. And the cost savings we realized for our clients were sometimes *half* of our engineering cost. That's huge! The savings not only made the client happy but also enabled us to move on to the next project faster. Those cost savings were used as a selling tool for future clients. We could demonstrate that our "brains were turned on" to help the client save money and schedule. Simple is elegant!

That's why I advocate that you find the "artsy" types in your organization and box them in whenever you can. Often, you don't need to build a better mousetrap; you just need to use the one that has been proven to work.

ELIMINATE WASTE EVERYWHERE YOU CAN

Finally, keep your eyes open for where people are doing things that aren't a good use of their time. They may not even realize this, so a fresh set of eyes always helps. Or they might—which likely frustrates them, because they can't figure out (or someone won't authorize) a more efficient way of working. It generally feels to me like there is up to 30 percent wasted effort in all areas of companies. Find it and fix it! Your people can help you do this.

I've mentioned my son's business, Fab Fours, Inc., which makes after-market replacement bumpers and accessories for trucks and jeeps. The first time I had a tour of his manufacturing plant, I noticed that the welders seemed to spend a lot of time just moving parts around, rather than actually welding. First, a welder needed to get a cart from the assembly line, bring all the pieces over, and start putting those pieces into a fixture to align them before he could start welding. Then, when he finished the welding on that bumper, he had to lift it off, put it back on the cart, and push the cart back into the assembly line for the next operator. All that moving back and forth from one area to another populating the fixture and doing other tasks was actually consuming about 50 percent of the welder's day. Obviously, that's not an efficient use of time for the highest-paid worker on the manufacturing floor.

In our industry, the same thing happened to the designers who created our drawings. When they do piping designs, for example, they need to know all the dimensions and a lot of other information for the instrumentation and valves that would go into those designs. Years ago (before all that information was on a computer), that meant they needed to get up from their desks and go look for that data in catalogs or other reference books or files, then return to their desks once they had the data they needed. Now they can search catalogues online, but it is still time consuming, and they may pick the wrong item.

We called this "monkey motion"—any activity where people have to go looking for information or parts or equipment that will *help* them do their jobs, but which also *takes time away from actually doing their jobs.* Whenever we saw this, we tried to streamline or eliminate it.

To make the designers more efficient, we realized that the instrument engineers who were specifying the control valves, for example, were looking right at the data for that valve, with all the dimensions and other information that the designers would need later and were spending so much time looking for. So, we simply asked the instrument engineers to make a copy of the page that had all the dimensions on it, highlight the correct information, and put it in a notebook that went to the designers. This way, they didn't have to leave their desks. Similarly, we asked the designers to add to that notebook any information they included in the design. So, anyone who was involved in that design would have all the information used to create it in a single place. And there didn't need to be a lot of back-and-forth questioning among departments to make sure that everything was accurate: all the information was right there.

Sounds ridiculously simple, right? That's because it is! Furthermore, with computers, this is even easier, because there is no physical notebook; there's simply a digital version. The concept is the same—but keep in mind that it only works if everyone involved uses and updates it, so that no one has to go around searching for the original data. This has to become a habit to create smooth handoffs between departments.

Similarly, to make the welder in my son's company more efficient, all he needed to do was take time-lapse photography to see how much of the day is spent actually welding. And it might be 50 percent of the time, but the welder is the most highly trained person and therefore the most expensive person on the team. So, if you can hire a lower paid person to *assist* the welder—for example, to move carts or equipment, to help install the parts onto the fixture for multiple welders, to sweep up—then you can increase the time the welder spends welding from 50 percent to 85 percent of the day. Perhaps you can hire fewer welders because they'll be more efficient.

Every organization has those bottlenecks; sometimes, it takes a fresh set of eyes to see where they are and how they can be removed. Look around your organization and see where there is wasted time, and if you can't think of an immediate fix, ask your people to brainstorm ways that can make themselves more efficient and productive.

OBJECTIVE:

Break the code on better execution with a repeatable process to become a Culture Code Champion. The increased efficiency will win more work for your people and pump up your bottom line.

EXECUTE: ESTABLISH A REPEATABLE PROCESS

KEY POINTS TO KEEP IN MIND ON EXECUTION:

1. Eliminate boom and bust cycles in your organization. *You may not have control over what's happening in your industry or the world in general, but you can still try to maintain an even flow of work. Develop a "No Fate" leadership mentality and know that the industry does not care if you survive. It is up to you.*

2. Work hardest at the beginning of a project. *In accordance with the project influence curve, you have the greatest ability to affect project outcomes (cost, schedule, quality, safety) early ... when costs are small.*

3. Name your repeatable process. *This will differentiate your company and help your people explain your process to new hires, suppliers, and clients. Win the communication battle; improve handoffs and use the name in hard copy communication.*

4. Utilize a work breakdown structure to "eat the elephant one bite at a time." *Implement "stage-gate" approach to project management, which requires a design freeze at each stage. This ensures the project doesn't get ahead of decisions— causing problems later in the schedule, when they are more difficult and expensive to correct.*

5. Reverse-plan projects. *Instead of scheduling projects chronologically from the start date, begin with the end date. Determine the desired end-state and backward plan from there. Identify ways to mitigate risk at each step. What are the critical handoffs that need to be worked?*

6. Don't let creative people get too creative. *We call this "boxing in the artsy folks," which every organization has. These people want to create everything from scratch, or work with the newest technologies or latest gadgets and equipment, when the tried-and-true will get the job done. Apply the KISS principle ... Keep It Super Simple. Think—bespoke with a manufacturing mentality.*

7. Always have a kickoff meeting. *Bring past work that might reduce the effort on the new project—we call these "go-bys." Strive to be 30 percent complete after the kickoff meeting.*

8. Be on the lookout for "monkey motion." *This is any activity that isn't directly linked to someone's primary responsibility, but which many people can spend up to 50 percent of their time on. Evaluate if something adds value or not. Find out where the wasted time is, and then eliminate it by reconfiguring your workspace, your process, or your staffing.*

CULTURE CODE CHAMPIONS WORKSHEET: STEP 3: ESTABLISH A REPEATABLE PROCESS

STRENGTH:
Internal:_____
_____

WEAKNESS:
Internal:_____
_____

OPPORTUNITY:
External:_____
_____

THREAT:
External:_____
_____

CHAMPION:
Hand Step 3 baton to: _____
    Buddy: _____
Conceptual initial actions:
    1. _____
    2. _____
    3. _____
    4. _____
Start Date: _____

CHAPTER 7

GIVE BACK: BE A COMMUNITY CHAMPION

Throughout this book, I've described the reasons my co-founders and I started our own company and the values and core philosophy (about business and life) that we shared. Those beliefs also extended to our ideas about giving back.

Once people feel more secure in their own lives, they often look to see how they can help others. Our culture gave them that feeling of security, and they started to give back to people who were less fortunate in our community. Like our other outside activities, our giving created leadership opportunities and "free space" for people to interact across the company. This chapter describes some of what we did—and our goal is to inspire you and your team to think of how *you* can give something back to your community.

HELPING FAMILIES IN NEED

We had been a company for less than six months when Joyce Covington, the wife of one of our co-founders, heard about two families that needed help at Christmastime. She asked if the company could pitch in and help, and our people bought those families everything on their wish list. Little did we know how that simple act of charity would grow! Mustangers were so energized by that experience that we started to reach out in many more ways.

Over the years, we worked with community centers, churches, food banks, organizations that worked with veterans and homeless people, and many more.

In some cases, our volunteers took the kids out shopping. For example, one year, a group of Young Guns—people working in our company who were still in their twenties—had chosen to buy things for a family that had a teenage boy, who had only listed clothes on his Christmas wish list. The young men in this group, who were only a decade older than this boy, realized that no teenage boy wants someone *else* to buy his clothes for him.

THINK OUTSIDE THE TOY BOX AND LOOK FOR MORE SUBSTANTIAL WAYS TO HELP FAMILIES.

So, they took the boy shopping. By the end of the shopping day, he had bonded with a few of the guys, and they stayed in touch with him afterward, to see how he was doing from time to time.

Think outside the toy box and look for more substantial ways to help families. Over the years, our giving expanded to include food, appliances—especially washers and dryers—and even furniture. In some cases, we helped by paying rent or utilities, if that's what would help a particular family most. We delivered the gifts personally to the families whenever possible.

It was a learning experience for our children, too. That first Christmas, I went with my wife and our eight-year-old son, and when our daughter was six, she came with us. We went into neighborhoods that some people had never been to: the unseen poverty that exists, sadly, in every American city and town.

WORKING WITH THE COMMUNITY TO BUILD HOMES AND HELP IN SCHOOLS

After a few years, we started working with the city of Houston on some of its projects. Similar to Habitat for Humanity (which we also worked with), the Private Sector Initiative (PSI) helped repair Houston homes. PSI supplied all materials needed. One of our designers, Henry Gomez, got us involved with this cause: it was something he found that his family wanted to be part of, and he felt he had the time to organize it. Just like our rabble rousers, who organized the fun events, some people took it upon themselves to organize our charitable work.

These home-repair projects were like old-fashioned barn raisings. As the old saying goes, *many hands make light work.* About sixty to eighty people volunteered—including entire families—on a Saturday, and we did anything and everything that needed to be done inside and outside the home, including landscaping. Our company supplied the lunch for all the volunteers, and we ate, picnic style, outside, under the trees. It was great fun, built camaraderie and was very worthwhile.

In 2004, we started a group within our company called Founders' Legacy to partner with junior high schools. We "adopted" one school for a few years and then rotated to another one. We collected school supplies, held lunches for the teachers, and mentored students. Some of the mentoring involved tutoring; in other situations, the mentors simply had lunch with a student to give him or her someone to talk with. Everyone could feel the impact of our help.

GIVING FROM THE HEART OF YOUR ORGANIZATION

In 2006, we created a name and logo for our charitable work. These initiatives became the "Heart of Mustang" program. The name summed up what we were doing, because we were really volunteering from our hearts.

Our charitable efforts expanded beyond simply buying and repairing things for others; we also helped families in longer-term ways. We tutored children in the home and helped their parents find better jobs by preparing resumes, helping them with the search, and practicing interviews.

Our volunteer work was organized *in addition* to the work everyone was responsible for. People spent significant time on these volunteer activities—sometimes as much as 10 percent of their workweeks—but that 10 percent was *on top of* the hours they were already working. They did this during lunchtime, before work, after work, and on the weekends, simply because they *wanted to*.

Even our clients and suppliers got involved and contributed to our efforts; there were countless examples from many companies, but one that stands out in my mind is when Chevron donated fifty bicycles to give to local families through the "Heart of Mustang."

RAISING MONEY TO SUPPORT CHARITABLE WORK

Throughout the year, our company held various fund-raising events. In addition, individual departments did their own fund-raising activities.

One year, we held a casino night to raise money. Again, this was another way to have fun outside of work, while raising money for a good cause. That became an annual event, and just a few years later, we raised $5,000, which enabled us to help seventeen families at Christmastime. We also held auctions and had barbecues.

In 2005, some of our people raised and donated $11,000 to the Red Cross Asian Tsunami Relief Fund. That same year, the company raised and donated $95,000 to help Mustangers who suffered losses during Hurricanes Katrina and Rita. In 2017, we donated more than $100,000 for the Harvey victims, mobilized crews to muck out over fifty homes, donated meals, and housed people temporarily while supporting "Hope after Harvey."

SENSE OF TEAM AND BONDING OPENS PEOPLE TO BECOME HEROES

One of the reasons our people felt that they *could* be so giving was because they finally felt *secure* about their own financial well-being. Our company made it clear that we valued our people and wanted them to have long-term employment. Helping others also welded our teams tighter together. The summation of this effort became evident to me when spouses came up to me at our Christmas parties to tell me how this job and our company had changed their spouses for the better. Their spouses were happier and more involved with their families, and that feeling spread outward to their community as well. If you can do that in your organization, you can make heroes of your people.

OBJECTIVE:

Break the code on giving back to your community to become a Culture Code Champion. The camaraderie, team building and bonding achieved through these efforts will increase people's satisfaction with your company and be reflected in your bottom line.

CULTURE CODE CHAMPIONS WORKSHEET:
STEP 7: GIVE BACK TO YOUR COMMUNITY

STRENGTH:
Internal:_____

_____

WEAKNESS:
Internal:_____

_____

OPPORTUNITY:
External:_____

_____

THREAT:
External:_____

_____

CHAMPION:
Hand Step 7 baton to: _____

Buddy: _____

Conceptual initial actions:

1. _____

2. _____

3. _____

4. _____

Start Date: _____

MAKE HEROES IN YOUR ORGANIZATION

We sold Mustang in 2000 to the Wood Group, using a mergers and acquisitions team from Chase Bank. We called the process our "Adopt a Parent" program, because we did not want to lose the culture that had differentiated us in the industry. Going against the Chase team's advice, we issued a pamphlet and met with our people, on a Monday morning, to announce that we wanted to sell the company and why. We wanted our people to know before anyone else. Usually, even the hint of the sale of a firm leads to good people "jumping ship" and clients stopping awards of work until the dust settles, and they can re-evaluate the capability of the new company. This is normal risk-avoidance for clients and people. The next day, on Tuesday, we announced to our clients and suppliers, in person or through email, our intention to sell and why. Then we held our breath and waited for the hurricane of activity.

And then ... nothing happened!

Word came back from around the world that we had a good transition plan that made sense for a thousand-person company that was moving strongly into international work and mega-projects. The overriding comment was "This makes sense; please do not mess it up."

During that same timeframe, two of the largest Engineering and Construction (E&C) companies had a strategic priority of winning the BP Deepwater contract (of approximately a billion dollars) to do four record-breaking drilling and production facilities in the Gulf of Mexico. Different partners on these four projects were Shell, Chevron, Unocal, BHP and Exxon, so all the major oil companies were involved. The two E&C houses had good contacts in these oil companies, from the boardrooms to the purchasing agents, and their strategies pulled on every relationship to win this work. At Mustang we called this "zippering" a client from top to bottom with your people. The C-suites of the two E&Cs were focused on delivering this win in 2000.

Halfway through the process of selling our company, we won the contract—the biggest reimbursable contract award in the industry, even as of this writing. During the meeting to sign the contract with members of all four project teams, we asked what differentiated us in their minds to pick Mustang. The program director said that whoever won the contract would have to hire hundreds of people, due to the size of these projects, and his team agreed that our culture allowed us to hire and develop strong teams better than the other competitors. **This was the most vivid example of "culture eating strategy for breakfast" that we ever witnessed!**

That is the destiny I want for you in whatever job you have.

Building strong teams gets the best out of individuals, and they develop tight relationships. These relationships lead to less turnover, as work becomes fun and challenging with the interpersonal team dynamics. Better efficiency and lower turnover leads to higher profits and a sustainable company through all business cycles. Building this team culture can be monetized, and even with today's dispersed workforce, it is achievable.

As employees become increasingly focused on finding meaning and making an impact instead of working only for traditional financial incentives, culture creation is even more important. Creating the sense of belonging to a team that is productive both at work and in the community will attract and help you keep the type of people you want.

To summarize what has been presented on building a high-performance team culture, here are the 7 Steps to Scale and Succeed in your business that you should implement. Assigning a champion to each one to get it started and keep pushing until the flywheel gets going is critical. Each of these steps must become a habit and part of the fabric of your organization:

- **Step 1—Open up the Communication.** Effective teamwork requires good communication, and lots of it, throughout your organization, as well as with your vendors, suppliers, clients and customers. It helps you make heroes of everyone your teams touch. Don't let your people shut themselves off in their offices and workspaces, and don't create such a hierarchy that people can communicate only through preapproved channels. Bust silos wherever they crop up. Help your people get to know each other—and their families—by providing free space where people can mingle and interact, either by doing charity events in the community or through parties or picnics or activities throughout the year, not only during holidays. Create fun, positive memories and smiles. Be inclusive by inviting your suppliers and clients into your company and culture to form a broader industry team. Look for ways to develop a "blue layer" in the organization to work across the inevitable silos and create efficiencies through better communication.

- **Step 2—Create a Sense of Team.** Create a fun identify for your organization that your people can rally around. Most people want to belong to something—and if they don't want that, they probably won't fit into your organization! Make up a name that people will use to identify themselves as part of the team. Develop mottos that sum up your organization's culture. Choose a mascot, like sports teams do. Preserve your company's history and stories, so all newcomers can share in what everyone else already knows. Create branded swag and give it out to everyone, often, not only at special occasions: this can be T-shirts, hats, banners, calendars, toys, anything. Brand it and distribute it, to keep people talking and thinking about your organization and its unique identity. Create energy and enthusiasm by putting smiles on people's faces and creating lasting memories ... be the team others want to join! And make sure you do this from day one with new hires, so they'll feel—and become—part of the team right away.

- **Step 3—Establish a Repeatable Process.** Eliminate waste and improve efficiency by streamlining as much as possible. Break projects into tasks and break tasks into smaller pieces. Start with the end in mind and backward plan. Follow the project influence curve's imperative to work hardest at the beginning of a project so there won't be any unpleasant surprises at the end! You want to be "bespoke with a manufacturing mentality." Work hard to set up both sides of every handoff required to get it right the first time and squeeze them for the "free money and time" that is available. Through cross-training, work to make all eyes informed eyes to catch errors early. A key success factor will be your ability to box in the artsy part of your company or organization to deliver quality on time. Name and brand your repeatable process for more ownership and to differentiate from your competitors.

- **Step 4—Use Hard Copy Communication.** Mailing the monthly newsletter home to pull the spouse and kids into the company culture is a simple thing to do that will weld your families into the company family you are working to create. Use your sales and marketing people to help with In-house sales to pull your people tighter together. This is mainly done through hard copy. Start at the coffee bar with fun pictures and announcements instead of government regulations ... spiral attitudes up before people walk back down the hall. Think about the opportunities you have: signs in the parking garage, in the stairwells, in conference rooms. Other key pieces of hard copy communications are Planner Pads, Miller Heiman Bluesheets® for sales, OZ® Accountability packets, checklists, proposals, etc. All of these can be nudges to build your culture of taking care of people and delivering on promises. Use Culture Code Champion batons to hand off each of the seven steps to your designated champions and start creating your new destiny.

- **Step 5—Sell While the Shop is Full.** People need to have a steady stream of work to feel secure in their jobs. Steady work for steady people is a great motto. The "job on the corner of the desk" goal helps foster security, because when people know there's another project waiting for them, they're likely to work harder and smarter to finish the task or project they're working on. Sell while the shop is full, to keep projects coming in and create a slight overload to increase efficiency. Make your company impossible to forget, so clients will call you first when they need help. Win the ties with your competitors by differentiating yourself and your organization. Remember, energy and enthusiasm is a force multiplier! Get your suppliers to help you through the use of "same sentence sales" to get in the door early. Create team sales in your organization by using a recognized sales process like Miller Heiman®. You want "No Fate Leadership" where you do not follow industry cycles up and down ... only up! Continuous sales will create job security, which allows a culture to blossom.

- **Step 6—Continuously Recruit Top Talent.** Recruiting and "high grading" your talent in good times and bad is a game changer as your talented people *are* your reputation. Referral hiring of people recommended by your people generally gives the best result as they will have your "DNA" ... remember to work hardest during the hiring and onboarding process for success down the line. Rectify your hiring mistakes as soon as you recognize them. Create a "Young Guns" program to grow new capability. Implement your own "operation horsethief" to identify the talent you need and then go get it. Once you have them, use the other culture steps to insure they do not leave, and you will see your bottom line grow.

- **Step 7—Give Back to Your Community.** There are virtually unlimited ways available to your organization to give back. Let your people pick ways that interest them and give them support. These activities will help develop leaders of character, open up communication across many boundaries, and help you build a stronger organization.

One of your Big Hairy Audacious Goals (BHAGs from Jim Collins's book *Good to Great*) should be to have culture as a differentiator both internally and externally. Put it in your SWOT (strength, weaknesses, opportunities, and threats) analysis and work on it. If you are not investing in your culture … I guarantee your culture is costing you.

Celebrate what you want to see more of as you assign a champion to develop each of the seven steps in building a winning people-focused culture. It will be very satisfying to see your teams and leaders grow.

Take what you have learned here to make heroes of everyone you come in contact with and remember to make your culture count!

I experienced high-performing teams and a winning culture at West Point and in the army. My partners experienced the unbeatable Texas A&M "Aggie" culture that welded people together for life. We brought those experiences and the Golden Rule (basically, treat others the way you would like to be treated) to the business world using the simple steps and building blocks above. The team culture that ensued changed lives positively by lifting people up and Making Heroes.

You can do it, too!

CULTURE CODE CREED

GIVE BACK TO YOUR COMMUNITY	07
CONTINUOUSLY RECRUIT TOP TALENT	06
SELL WHILE THE SHOP IS FULL	05
USE HARD COPY COMMUNICATION	04
ESTABLISH A REPEATABLE PROCESS	03
CREATE A SENSE OF TEAM	02
OPEN UP THE COMMUNICATION	01

above the line

CULTURE KILLERS

below the line

Not being other-oriented

Hiring available, average talent

Stop selling when overloaded

Relying on digital copy only

Starting anything from scratch

Going it alone

Turf building

ACKNOWLEDGEMENTS

My wife's work ethic and encouragement gave me the freedom to throw myself wholeheartedly into Mustang. My partners Paul Redmon, Felix Covington, and their wives, provided unconditional support for our mission to create a company built around making heroes. My children, Greg and Stephanie, have always kept me grounded through the ups and downs of life and business.

Thousands of Mustangers touched the flywheel every day to build the cultural momentum that changed our destiny in the industry. Leaders in the Boy Scouts, coaches, pastors, and teachers throughout school, West Point classmates, leaders at Ranger School and in the army, and industry colleagues all helped me learn how to be other-oriented. This book is the reflection of all these people's influences on me and I thank them immensely.

MAKING HEROES

WHAT IS YOUR CURRENT CULTURE COSTING YOU?

MAKE YOUR CULTURE COUNT!

VISIT: CULTURECODECHAMPIONS.COM

ABOUT THE AUTHOR

Bill Higgs and two partners started Mustang Engineering, Inc. in Houston, Texas, in 1987 to design and build industrial facilities. Over the next twenty years, they grew the company from their initial $15,000 investment and three people to a billion-dollar company with 6,500 people worldwide. Since then, it has grown to a $2 billion company with more than 12,000 people. Mustang won the "Innovate Houston" award for being the most people-oriented company in Houston. This award confirmed the "People Oriented ... Project Driven™" motto of Mustang and affirmed Bill's passion for team-building and organizational development.

Mustang developed a culture that helped retain people and deliver top performance on first-of-a-kind projects around the world. The industry labeled the founders the "Kings of Culture" worldwide and awarded them their Lifetime Achievement Award for "Visionary Leadership in the Process Industries."

Since retiring from Mustang Engineering, Bill has consulted for other companies and given speeches, worldwide, on project management and culture. Bill was selected as a Forbes Author and a Forbes Speaker in 2018. He has led Vistage and Entrepreneur Organization sessions on culture development since 2016 and has consulted with various companies on culture development since 2014.

He is on the advisory board for Arion, a firm that started in Houston in 2017 and was patterned on Mustang. Since 2005, he has been a board member of Fab Fours, a 130-person steel manufacturing plant; he also serves on the board of the Mecklenburg Council of the Boy Scouts of America and the National Council for STEM education. He is the author of *Mustang, The Story: from Zero to $1 Billion,* published in 2016.

Bill spent 1980 fighting Stage IV cancer. After surgery and radiation, he was treated with experimental chemotherapy due to the aggressive nature of the cancer. Through the yearlong cancer fight, he was grateful for the high-performance team at MD Anderson Cancer Center.

He is a distinguished 1974 graduate (top 5 percent academically) of the United States Military Academy at West Point and runner up for a Rhodes scholarship. He lettered two years in Division 1 soccer as the center fullback of a defense that set the school shutout record. He was also on the intercollegiate wrestling and judo teams. Bill was honor graduate of the Army Ranger School and "king of the pits" in hand-to-hand combat. After Airborne and Atomic Demolitions courses, he commanded a combat engineering company in the First Cavalry Division and was honorably discharged as a captain in 1979.

Bill grew up in scouting and earned his Eagle Scout badge with three palms. He continues to be involved in the Boy Scouts, serving on regional boards in Houston and Charlotte, North Carolina. He has received the Distinguished Eagle and Silver Beaver awards for service to the Boy Scouts of America.

Bill was born in Denver, Colorado; raised in Cleveland, Ohio; and spent thirty years in Houston, Texas, before moving with his wife, Ann, to Charlotte, North Carolina, in 2006.

JOIN THE DISCUSSION & MAKE YOUR CULTURE COUNT!

Tune in to the Culture Code Champions Podcast hosted by Bill Higgs and discover how entrepreneurs can make it big with PEOPLE-ORIENTED BUSINESS SUCCESS. Bill interviews the world's top leaders in business, entrepreneurship as well as global thought leaders that share their first hand experience, knowledge, and wisdom to give you exclusive access to their secrets for success.

If you've cracked the code to culture and have had great business success, BOOK AN INTERVIEW WITH BILL:
www.interviewwithbill.com

www.culturecodechampionspodcast.com